the Institute *of* Public Relations

P R   I N   P R A C T I C E   S E R I E S

PLANNING & MANAGING A PUBLIC RELATIONS CAMPAIGN

A step-by-step guide

Anne Gregory

the Institute *of* Public Relations

KOGAN PAGE

The Institute of Public Relations (IPR)

The IPR is the professional body for public relations in the UK. Its role is:
- to provide a professional structure for the practice of public relations;
- to enhance the ability and status of its members as professional practitioners;
- to represent the interests of its members;
- to provide opportunities for members to meet and exchange views and ideas;
- to offer a range of services of professional and personal benefit to members.

Founded in 1948, the Institute now has over five thousand four hundred members practising in consultancies and in-house in all sectors of the UK economy. Members, whether generalist or specialist, are drawn from all areas of practice and management, up to main Board level, in industry and commerce, local and central government, in health and education services and charities, in the police and armed forces, in privatised and nationally owned utilities and services.

Membership of the Institute of Public Relations

Since January 1992 full membership (MIPR) of the Institute has been gained only by qualification combined with a period of professional experience, although for senior practitioners the qualification element may be substituted by ten years experience. The criteria established for the qualification element is to reach, both in range and depth, the standards laid down in the Public Relations Education and Training Matrix.

One consequence of this decision is that, increasingly over time, membership will comprise practitioners and managers who have a formally recognised public relations qualification.

The Institute also offers Student membership and Associate membership (AMIPR) for those on their way to full membership. Affiliate membership is for those who work in a specialised area of communication and who support the Institute's aims, but who would not be entitled to full membership. Fellowship (FIPR) is awarded to Members in recognition of outstanding work in public relations.

For further information please contact:

The Institute of Public Relations
The Old Trading House
15 Northburgh Street
London EC1V 0PR
Tel: 0171 253 5151
Fax: 0171 490 0588

the Institute *of* Public Relations

PR IN PRACTICE SERIES

PLANNING & MANAGING A PUBLIC RELATIONS CAMPAIGN

A step-by-step guide

170101

YOURS TO HAVE AND TO HOLD
BUT NOT TO COPY

First published in 1996, reprinted 1997 and 1998

Kogan Page Limited
120 Pentonville Road
London N1 9JN

© Anne Gregory, 1996

British Library Cataloguing in Publication Data
A CIP record for this book is available from the British Library.

ISBN 0 7494 1858 3

Typeset by BookEns Ltd, Royston, Herts.
Printed and bound in Great Britain by Biddles Ltd, Guildford and King's Lynn

Contents

PR in Practice Series

Published in association with the Institute of Public Relations
Consultant Editor: Anne Gregory

Kogan Page has joined forces with the Institute of Public Relations to publish this unique new series which is designed specifically to meet the needs of the increasing numbers of people seeking to enter the public relations profession and the large band of existing PR professionals.

Taking a practical, action-oriented approach, the books in the series will concentrate on the day-to-day issues of public relations practice and management rather than academic theory.

They will provide ideal primers for all those on IPR, CAM and CIM courses or those taking NVQs in PR. For PR practitioners, they will provide useful refreshers and ensure that their knowledge and skills are kept up-to-date.

Anne Gregory is head of the School of Business Strategy and an assistant dean of the Faculty of Business at Leeds Metropolitan University. As former chair of the Institute of Public Relations' Education and Training Committee, Anne initiated the PR in Practice series.

Forthcoming titles in the series are:

> *Effective Media Relations*
> Michael Bland, Alison Theaker and David Wragg
> *A Practitioner's Guide to Implementing Public Relations*
> Philip Henslowe
> *Public Relations in Practice*
> Edited by Anne Gregory
> *Running a Public Relations Consultancy*
> Peter Hehir
> *Running a Public Relations Department*
> Mike Beard
> *Strategic Public Relations*
> Edited by Carol Friend

Available from all good bookshops, or to obtain further information please contact the publishers at the address below:

Kogan Page Ltd
120 Pentonville Road
London N1 9JN
Tel: 0171 278 0433
Fax: 0171 837 6348

Acknowledgements

In drawing up a list of those organisations and individuals who must be thanked for helping with the writing of this book, it is very difficult to know where to start.

First of all there are all the organisations I have worked for and with whom over the years I have built up my knowledge and experience of public relations to an extent where this book was possible.

Then there are those who have generously supplied me with materials, including the Institute of Public Relations (I have borrowed shamelessly from their Awards of Excellence), Pilkington PLC, Maria Darby of Lansons Communications and Carol Friend of Peille. Special thanks go to Professor Tim Traverse-Healy and the Distance Learning Programme at Stirling University for permission to use ideas taken from materials prepared by Ann Dunne, Sam Black, Danny Moss, Don Bathie and George Panigyrakis.

I would like to thank the public relations students at Leeds Metropolitan University for whom I prepared materials on planning and managing public relations, and who stimulated my thinking.

I am very grateful to Ruth Parkinson and to Dr Jon White for their most helpful comments on the draft of this book, and to Narinder Uppal who painstakingly word-processed it for me.

To the IPR/Kogan Page Editorial Board of Christopher Ashton-Jones, Dick Fedorcio, Carol Friend, Michael Regester, John Lavelle, Philip Mudd, Pauline Goodwin and Tony Mason, many thanks for your encouragement and support.

To Mark, for his patient listening, sound counsel and several late nights.

About the author

Anne Gregory is Head of the School of Business Strategy and an Assistant Dean of the Faculty of Business at Leeds Metropolitan University.

Before entering academic life in 1991 she spent ten years in public relations at a senior level both in-house and in consultancy. Her last full-time position was as a director for Paragon Communications based in Leeds.

At Leeds Metropolitan University Anne ran the undergraduate public relations course between 1991 to 1995 on which she still teaches. She maintains a lively interest in public relations practice and is regularly involved in consultancy work.

As chair of the Institute of Public Relations' (IPR) Education and Training Committee, Anne initiated the IPR/Kogan Page series of books on public relations.

1

Planning and managing can be fun!

Everyone can plan and manage

Mention the words 'planning' or 'managing' to some people, particularly if they are creative, and they are immediately struck with horror.

On the other hand, some 'management types' like to surround the words with a great mystique. Only certain kinds of people are capable of doing such lofty activities, but most of us have to be content with carrying out the instructions of those who know about these things.

This is rubbish! Everyone is capable of planning and managing – we all do it all the time. We plan our home lives – what to eat and when, especially if we're having friends round. We plan holidays, how to spend Christmas, how to make large purchases and how to manage the conflicting demands of various members of the family whether they live with us or not.

Work and social life demands planning to a greater or lesser extent. Sometimes this planning is formal; sometimes it's just a pattern we follow when we repeat a familiar task. Certainly if we want to be in charge of our lives, and given the pace of change and activity, we need to plan to fit everything in and give ourselves space to have some fun.

And that is at the heart of planning and management. We don't do it to make our lives over-regulated and predictable, we do it to ensure everything is done that needs to be done, to create space and to put us in control. We drive events instead of being driven by them.

Planning and managing things properly can be exciting. It's a creative process. It's a process that stimulates our intellect, can bring great satisfaction and by harnessing various techniques we can ensure we are more effective and efficient in the way we work.

Planning in public relations

A good starting point when thinking about public relations and planning is to look at some of the recent definitions of public relations. According to the UK's Institute of Public Relations:

> Public relations practice is the planned and sustained effort to establish and maintain goodwill and mutual understanding between an organisation and its publics.

At the heart of this definition is the notion that public relations has to be planned. It is a deliberate, carefully thought-out process. It also requires ongoing (sustained) activity which is not haphazard. The activity is concerned with initiating (establishing) and maintaining a process of mutual understanding. In other words it involves a dialogue where an organisation and its various publics seek to listen to each other and understand each other.

Implicit in all this is that public relation practitioners are carefully considering how programmes need to begin, and continue in a structured way to the benefit both of their organisation and to the 'publics' their organisation interacts with.

More recent definitions by the IPR state that:

> Public relations is about reputation – the result of what you do, what you say and what others say about you.

and

> Public relations practice is the discipline which looks after reputation with the aim of earning understanding and support and influencing opinion and behaviour.

A good reputation is not something that is earned overnight. It has to be carefully and considerately cultivated. It is something that is earned over a period of time as understanding and support develops for an organisation. The management of reputation has to be carefully undertaken with integrity and honesty. It is something that is very fragile and can be lost quickly if words or actions are found to be out of sympathy with reality, or if careless talk gets out of hand. There is no better example of that than Gerald Ratner's comments about the jewellery in his chain of shops being 'crap'.

On the other hand the careful handling by Rolls-Royce Motors and Marks and Spencer of their reputations means that they have enjoyed public esteem for many years. The reality of their spoken, public claims is borne out by their actual products and services.

A virtuous circle is created where a good reputation raises expectations about the kind of products or services a company supplies and the quality of the products or services enhances the reputation.

Public relations has a job of work to do

All this means that public relations has a real job of work to do. It has to contribute directly to business success. If its task is guarding and managing reputation and relationships this must have a demonstrable effect, and not just result in a 'feel-good' factor. Spending money on establishing a dialogue with key publics and building a reputation has to result in tangible benefits to the organisation. Publics are influenced in their favour.

Ongoing research by MORI (MORI Corporate Image Study) demonstrates the power of reputation. Its 1994 survey showed that:

- 60 per cent of the general public believe 'A company with a good reputation would not sell poor products';
- 31 per cent say they would 'never buy products made by companies they had not heard of';
- 46 per cent think 'old established companies make the best products'.

If a company has a good reputation the evidence is that people are:

- more likely to try its new products;
- more likely to buy its shares;
- more likely to believe its advertising;
- more likely to want to work for it.

Establishing and maintaining a good reputation with key publics is a meticulous, time and energy-consuming business, requiring all the skills and attributes of planners and managers of the highest calibre. To be involved with building the reputation of a company is quite an awesome task.

The role of public relations in business

To understand how public relations programmes and campaigns are planned and managed, it is first essential to understand the role of public relations in business.

It is not the aim of this book to go into the detail of how organisations are structured and managed, and how they function. There are many excellent text books on this. It is, however, incumbent on all public relations practitioners to understand these issues otherwise they will not be able to fulfil their proper role within their organisation.

Simply put, an organisation consists of three elements:

- fixed assets such as its buildings, office furniture, car fleet and products;
- liquid assets or the money which lubricates the business; and
- people.

Its fixed assets have a finite value and can be accounted for on a balance sheet. Similarly, the amount of liquid assets an organisation has can be accounted for. It is obvious that the number of people that work for an organisation can be counted, but in many ways employees are an unquantifiable asset. Their capabilities are basically unbounded. They are the ones who put life into an organisation to create added value. They are the ones who use their creativity and ingenuity to design new products and sell them. They provide the customer service. They make organisations work. Assets, whether fixed or liquid, on their own are neutral commodities.

Furthermore, people interact with other people who are not necessarily a part of the organisation. They create customer relationships, they have families and friends who may or who may not support their organisation. They deal with suppliers, with local and central government, with the local community and so on.

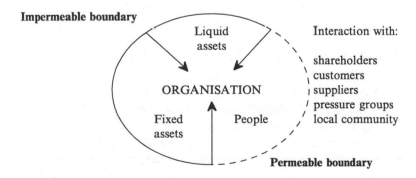

Figure 1.1 *How people extend the boundaries of an organisation*

People are an infinitely expandable resource and they blur the edges of an organisation's boundaries by drawing into the organisation other people, who strictly speaking are external to its operation. Furthermore, some employees are also members of groups external to the organisation, but critical to its success. As well as being employees, they can be customers, shareholders, and are probably members of the local community.

The main role of the chief executive of an organisation is to provide vision. They should have vision not only of how to do things well now, but most importantly for the future direction of the organisation. Badly managed organisations have no clear direction. They have no clear long-term objectives, but stumble along being constantly diverted to deal with the crises or apparent opportunities of the day without being focused on achieving their main, long-term objectives.

The role of the public relations professional within organisations

A seminal study by the International Association of Business Communicators (IABC), which began in 1987, asked the question 'What contribution does public relations make to an organisation's effectiveness?'

The study emphasises the contribution that public relations can make to the strategy of an organisation. An organisation's strategy (which determines long-term direction and scope) is determined after a great deal of analysis and decision-making. Many people, both outside and inside the organisation, will contribute to this process. Having developed a strategy, this will need to be communicated so that it can be supported and implemented. Public relations has an essential role to play in this process.

Communication is intelligence

First of all, the job of the public relations professional is to communicate with and build upon a relationship with all the organisation's publics. They are (or should be) acutely aware of the social environment in which the organisation operates and can supply that intelligence to the strategic planners. Because of their 'boundary spanning' role as conduits of information to publics inside and outside an organisation they can also act as information gatherers – drawing useful information together from their various publics and presenting that as useful intelligence.

Of course information about other contextual factors also needs to be obtained, for example economic and financial facts, and intelligence about technological developments. Often this information is gathered by specialists scattered throughout the organisation. The public relations function, because of its 'boundary spanning role', may be able to act as a central intelligence gathering function and, provided there are suitably trained specialists, supply an analysis and interpretation service too.

This strategic use of the public relations function implies that there is a recognition of its status by management. Public relations is more than a tactical tool used purely to 'communicate' information or add a gloss to information. It is an integral part of the strategic development process grounded on thorough-going research and skilled, objective analysis.

Some of the specialist contacts that the public relations function have are invaluable sources of early information and can pinpoint emerging issues that may have profound impact on an organisation. For example, media content analysis can identify the importance of an issue or the direction that public opinion is likely to take on an issue. Public affairs contacts can flag up government thinking on prospective legislation and city contacts can give early warning of likely investor activity.

By making sense of the environment, besides providing intelligence to the strategic development process, public relations professionals can contribute to the general decision-making within organisations. Because they have antennae that are alert to the external and internal environment that the organisation operates within, they can bring an invaluable, independent perspective to decision-making by managers who are often too close to a situation to act objectively or who are unaware of some of the ramifications of those decisions so as far as the outside world is concerned. It could well be that what on the face of it appears to be correct business decisions have to be questioned when they are set within a broader context. For example, it might make apparent business sense for an organisation to obtain supplies from the cheapest, most reliable source. But what if that source employs child labour?

There is therefore a two-fold role for the public relations professional here. First, it is to counsel management on the implications of its decisions, taking into account the likely reaction of key publics who directly affect the well-being or otherwise of a company. The public relations professional is the monitor of public opinion, and the conscience and ethical mentor of the organisation. Second, the public relations professional keeps senior management informed of what is happening in the social environment, which is peopled by its stakeholders, so that this is taken into account as decisions are made. The communication process is two-way as Figure 1.2 shows.

Figure 1.2 *The two-way information flow between an organisation and its environment*

Communication skill

Once having determined strategy, this needs to be communicated. Public relations professionals can be used by senior management to advise on both the content of the communication itself and the mechanics to be used for relaying information to publics. Because strategic information and plans are so important, management are often tempted to communicate them in pompous language and in an inappropriate form, for example a highly glossy brochure that permits no discussion or questioning! The communication professional must resist such actions and provide skilled advice on how to undertake the communication task.

The very process of insisting that clear messages are relayed to important groups of people helps to put rigour into strategic thinking and decision-making. It helps to clear woolly thinking and forces management to think through the practical implications of their planning. It is possible to cloak reality behind fine-sounding words. Distilling ideas down to simple language provides a check on how realistic those ideas are and makes comparisons between what's said and what's done more simple. So, if the reality doesn't meet the claim, don't say it!

At a tactical level, the role of the public relations practitioner is to manage appropriate communication using whatever technique is most suitable and timely between an organisation and its stakeholders, and vice versa.

For example, shareholders will want to know about the future development plans of a company in some detail, including its overseas aspirations. How and when that information is relayed to them is very important. UK customers, on the other hand, are less likely to be so concerned about this. They will first want to know that a particular shop will be open next week or that a favourite product will continue to be available. The fact that the company plans to open outlets in Hong Kong or Singapore in 1999 will probably not concern them.

The importance of communication

So why is communication important?

First of all it helps to further the strategic objectives of an organisation because it seeks to enlist the support of all the various groups or key publics by ensuring the vision and values of the chief executive and organisation are clearly communicated. The point of the communication is not just passing on information about the vision, but to gain active pursuit of or at least assent to those objectives (depending on the public). The communication is designed to influence behaviour.

Of course, if the organisation listens as well as speaks and acts, its communication will have been affected by research undertaken with those key publics and will continue to be affected by them. It is, therefore, more likely to be effective in its communication.

Second it positively fosters relationships with key publics. These publics are ultimately responsible for the destiny of the organisation for good and ill. As a result of this, good communication enhances the opportunities that are presented to organisations by both identifying them early and facilitating the actions that are required to capitalise on them (whether this be a sales opportunity or an opportunity to influence legislation). It also helps minimise the threats by spotting problems or potential conflicts early (for example, identifying increasing employee disquiet or discontent with a proposed company action).

The position of public relations within organisations

More detailed information on the role of public relations practitioners is given in Chapter 2. At this stage it is important to look at the position and status that public relations occupies within organisations, since that is linked to its role as a strategic or tactical function.

A good indication of how public relations is regarded is to establish where the function is placed. If senior public relations managers are part of the 'dominant coalition'[1] of company

---

[1]From Grunig, J E and Hunt, T (1992) *Managing Public Relations*, Holt, Rinehart and Winston, 2nd edn.

decision-makers, then public relations is likely to serve a key strategic role. Those individuals are likely to undertake the research and counselling activities outlined below. If not, public relations is likely to be largely tactical. It could well be seen just as a part of the marketing communications mix or regarded as largely to do with presenting information about the organisation in an acceptable (usually to the organisation) way.

Another indication of how seriously the activity is taken is to gauge whether it is mainly reactive or proactive. Of course there is always a level of reactive public relations in any programme. However good the planning, the unexpected is likely to occur, whether that be a pressure group making an unexpected attack (justified or ill-founded) or another organisation making a takeover bid out of the blue. There are also opportunistic openings that should be grasped. It might be, for example, that there is an interest in the media over famine in Africa. If your organisation is a charity helping orphaned African children you would be provided with a golden opportunity to publicise your own work.

In organisations where public relations is taken seriously and proactively, it is normally found that the senior practitioner holds a major position in the organisation. They will provide a counselling role for fellow senior managers and directors, and they will have overall responsibility for the communication strategy of the organisation – that might include determining the key overall marketing, advertising and promotional strategy. It will certainly involve working very closely with those disciplines.

Activity will be directed at building reputation positively and will have a strategic purpose. Issues like social responsibility and corporate governance will be taken seriously. Programmes will be based on careful formal and informal research, and a knowledge of who the key publics are, how these publics regard the organisation and what they see as priorities. The programmes that are devised will be concerned with impact, and aim to influence attitudes, opinions and behaviours. They will not be obsessed with process such as how many news releases are produced, but the effectiveness of public relations activity will be closely monitored. Often these organisations will be industry leaders and setting the pace in the market. They will usually be the ones available to the media and seen to be the voice of their industry. They are on the whole open, communicative organisations.

In organisations where public relations is seen as a lower order activity and where its practice is normally reactive, certain tell-tale traits will be evident. The practitioner will not hold a senior management role and will not be involved in corporate decision-making. The task will be to respond to events and will often be defensive. The function will tend to communicate what has already happened, and the activity will be largely one-way with the organisation telling the world what it has done or is doing and not being influenced by what the world is saying to it. Any progress will be an evolution of what has happened in the past. The practitioner will not feel valued or in control and will not be a part of the 'dominant coalition'.

It is partly the public relations industry and individual practitioners who have encouraged this reactive, technical role for public relations. Too often public relations has been regarded as just media relations – free media publicity at that – or as just a part of marketing communication. The schematic in Figure 1.3 shows the relationship between public relations and marketing, and indicates the shared areas of activity and those areas where public relations has a quite separate remit.

Public relations practitioners also have only themselves to blame for not learning as much as they should about business and how it operates. How can they be at the decision-making table if they have no real grasp on what makes a business tick?

In his survey of public relations practitioners Turk[1] discovered that lack of financial and budgeting skills were perceived as being the greatest deficiency in practitioners. Other deficiencies were problem-solving and decision-making, goal-

---

[1] Turk, V J (1989) 'Management skills need to be taught in public relations', *Public Relations Review*, Spring, pp 38–52.

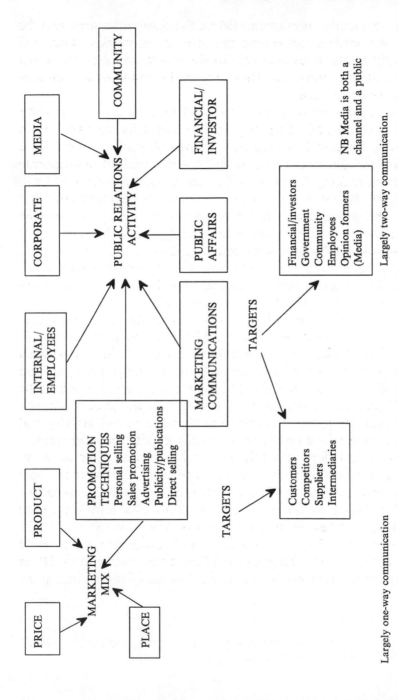

Figure 1.3 *The inter-relationship of public relations and marketing*

setting and prioritising, planning and organisation, analytical skills and time management.

To mature fully as a discipline public relations must take on the responsibilities of knowledge, planning and management just as any other business function.

2

The public relations function in context

Context is vitally important

Two books in this series, *Running a Public Relations Department* (to be published in June 1996) and *Running a Public Relations Consultancy* (to be published in October 1996), look in detail at how the public relations function should be organised both in-house and in consultancies.

However, to plan and manage campaigns effectively it is vitally important to look at the context in which public relations activity takes place, since this differs from organisation to organisation. It helps to look at the factors affecting organisations in a systematic way, and addressing the areas outlined in Figure 2.1 provides a blueprint for doing this.

This approach is not really research about specific public relations problems or opportunities (more of this in Chapter 3), but it is vital background information required to plan and manage effectively.

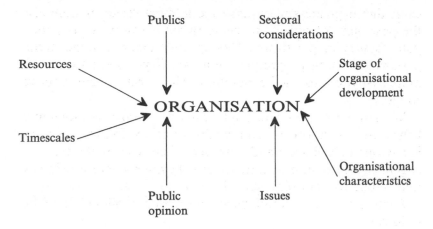

Figure 2.1 *Factors to be considered when researching the background for public relations activity.*

Publics

Chapter 6 has a much more detailed discussion of publics, but from the outset it is important that the public relations practitioner is aware of the whole range of publics that must be communicated with. This will be a major factor in deciding the public relations task. Each public will have a different communication requirement, although the information given to each must not conflict.

The object of the exercise is to enlist the support of these publics. Sometimes that support will need to be very active and immediate, for example you want customers to buy your products and shareholders to support your company activities by not selling their shares. Sometimes the support is less active and not bound by specific timescales. For example, you might organise a community relations campaign, simply because you feel it right to put something back into a community that provides most of your workforce. There might be no specific business objectives, but the feeling of goodwill that the campaign engenders may make recruitment easier or minimise the possibility of objections being raised if you want to extend your factory in the future. Having undertaken a longer-term, goodwill-building programme you can, if you need to, switch more easily to a focused programme which seeks to enlist active support.

With some publics you might want to change opinions and behaviour, with others you might want to confirm existing behaviour or opinions and with yet others you might want to engender an opinion or pattern of behaviour where previously that public was entirely neutral.

Factors to bear in mind when considering publics include the following.

- **Range.** That is the breadth of publics concerned. For some organisations, for example, manufacturers of highly specialised military components, the range of publics may be very small. For other organisations, for instance, the Department of Employment, the range of publics is very large indeed.

- **Numbers and location.** Some organisations have a range of publics that fall into large uniform blocks, for example, the multiple retailers will have large groups of customers, suppliers and local authorities as some of their audiences. Others, for example, project engineers will have a whole range of publics, often small in number, attached to each project. Some organisations have publics covering a wide geographical or socio-economic spread; others have very focused groups to concentrate on.

- **Influence and power.** Some publics, for example active pressure groups can gain a great deal of power, particularly if they catch the public mood. They may not be large in numbers or have any direct link to the organisation, but they can be highly influential over the way an organisation conducts its business. Shell's reversal of its decision to sink the Brent Spar oil platform in the North Sea was forced by a small, but highly effective organisation (Greenpeace) galvanising public opinion. In a different way, shareholders wield a great deal of power. They have an obvious stake in an organisation and can determine its future overnight. One of the tasks of the public relations practitioner is to determine the relative influence and power of all the publics concerned, and weight the public relations programme accordingly. This is not to say that the most important publics always need to have the most money spent on them, but obviously their concerns and communication needs are paramount.

- *Connection with organisation.* Some publics are intimately connected with an organisation, for example, its employees. Others have a more remote connection, for example members of the local community. Some publics will have an amicable relationship with the organisation, others will find themselves in opposition to it. Again, the public relations practitioner needs to have a clear perception of these relationships and to gauge their changing nature. Some relationships could be in danger of becoming distant or of deteriorating. Others, for example if the legitimate concerns of a pressure group are addressed, may ameliorate over time and indeed turn from negative to positive. Some groups are always active, some very rarely. Furthermore some publics may have very active sub-groups within them, whereas other sections of the same public may be apparently quiescent, but with the potential to become active. Shareholders are a classic example of this. Thus the needs not only of the whole group, but parts of it also need to be considered.

Sectoral considerations

The nature of the sector in which the organisation finds itself will profoundly influence the way public relations is conducted. Public relations for a market-leading manufacturer of fast moving consumer goods is quite different from undertaking public relations for a college of further education.

Each sector has its own particular opportunities, threats and constraints. The various sectors in the public or non-profit making area are:

- education;
- government;
- National Health Service (NHS) health and medical care;
- voluntary organisations;
- charities.

Some of the organisations in these sectors are enormous and the public relations support required for a major government department such as the Department of Health or a large international charity such as Oxfam are quite as large and complex as anything that would be found in the private sector. In fact, because of the constraints placed on some of those organisations, for example the requirements of the Citizen's Charter or the need to account for every single pound spent on promotional activity, the challenges can be seen to be greater than those in private industry where it could be argued there is less direct external accountability.

The private sector, too, cannot be regarded as a uniform mass. It can be split up into the following areas:

- commerce;
- finance;
- manufacturing;
- services;
- retail.

Working in the manufacturing environment where there may be great emphasis on marketing communication activities in the sales promotion area such as exhibitions, demonstrations, conferences etc can be quite different from working in commerce where the balance may be towards paper-based public relations describing various activities.

There is one other sector that does not fit neatly into either public or private and that is the professions, such as accountancy, law and medicine which straddle both.

Organisational development – business stage

Public relations activities are often dictated by the stage of development at which an organisation finds itself.

Development depends on the sort of industry an organisation operates within. For example in the fashion or in the hi-tech industries, development and decline can be very rapid indeed. Other industries, the motor trade or food retailing being cases in point, mature more slowly and then the position is maintained. Ford Motor Company is a good example of a mature, established company.

Then there are variations within industries. The computer company Microsoft has grown very rapidly in an industry that has been dominated for years by big names such as IBM and ICL.

Factors affecting organisational development are:

- the nature of the industry;
- competitor activity;
- technological impacts;
- management decisions on direction;
- resources, both financial and human.

Looking at the various stages of an organisation's development reveals that there will be specific public relations requirements at different times.

- *Start-up.* Usually companies start small. The owners will know suppliers, customers and their employees, and often there will not be a separate public relations function. Public relations will be in the form of one-to-one contact with the various publics, with maybe some literature to support the contact. The main emphasis will be on marketing communication since growth will be a priority.

- *Growth.* With more employees and more customers, face-to-face contact may not be possible and management time will be taken up managing the business. At this stage an individual public relations practitioner or a consultancy may be employed. Public relations will still be viewed quite narrowly, largely as a part of the marketing communication mix. Externally activity will focus on raising awareness of the company, and its products and services. Internally it may be that there would be the beginnings of a formal communication programme including briefings, use of internal memoranda, notice boards, social activities and so on.

The priority will be on expansion and capital costs could be quite high, especially if new premises have to be acquired. Resource constraints are likely to be a major factor influencing the role of public relations. Certainly activities like a comprehensive community relations programme are likely to be low on the agenda.

- *Maturity.* At this stage the organisation is likely to be well established. The public relations function probably will be expanded and certainly the range of activities it is involved in is likely to be considerably broadened.

  It could well be that a stockmarket flotation is being considered. Capital might be needed for expansion or acquisition. If this is the case an active financial public relations campaign will be pursued.

  Employee relations will be more developed. The objective will be to have an efficient and well-motivated workforce who are working to known organisational objectives and who help to maintain a competitive edge. There will also be the need to attract good quality new staff to the organisation.

  The employee relations programme will be well developed including techniques such as employee briefings, conferences, newsletters, video and e-mail communication. Public relations may be involved in supporting the training function in producing compact disc interactive (CD-I) training programmes, and indeed may be using CD-I itself in internal and external communication programmes.

  The public relations department may be assisted by one or more public relations consultancies and will be running a full corporate programme as well as continuing to support marketing efforts. The organisation should, at this stage, have a unified, cohesive identity and an established reputation. Furthermore it should have a developed sense of corporate responsibility, as it impacts more and more on the environment in which it operates (both local and remote). It will probably be involved actively in a range of community relations projects, including sponsorships, help in kind, support of local initiatives and so on.

- **Decline.** Many companies avoid decline by adjusting their orientation or by moving into new areas of activity. However, for whatever reason, takeover, financial or legislative change, or downright bad management, some organisations move into a period of temporary or permanent decline. There is a vital role for public relations to play. Spotting the issues before they become crises is a key role (see Chapter 4 for more on this). Handling crises with honesty and integrity if they do happen (for example a major product recall as in the case of Perrier, or a major incident such as the M1 plane crash for British Midland) can help maintain reputation and minimise the risk of a crisis unravelling out of control.

Ultimately if a business is non-viable, there is nothing public relations can do to rescue it. However, managing the expectations, and trying to influence the behaviour, of those publics critical to the eventual fate of an organisation in decline is very much within the remit of public relations. This is not a manipulative or unethical practice, but it is managing the situation professionally, bearing in mind the legitimate interests of all those involved.

Organisational characteristics

Knowing the organisation is imperative. There should be no skeletons unknown to the public relations practitioner, who should know the organisation inside out: history, its current status, its future plans, everything there is to know. The following headings give a framework for investigation.

- *Nature of organisation.* Know the sector. What are the trends for the industry? Is it expanding, contracting and are there new, exciting markets? What is the operating environment? Is the economy in recession and are there any major issues facing the industry or the company, such as new legislation or pressing environmental demands?

- *Competitor activity.* How is the organisation placed in relation to the competition? Is it possible to take market leadership in some or all areas? Are competitors new, aggressive young Turks likely to steal the market? Are there few or many competitors? Which ones are making headway and why? What are their weaknesses?

- *Mission.* What is the mission of the organisation? Is it to be the biggest, the best, the most innovative? Is it possible to be distinctive or will it be a 'Me too'? Is the mission realistic or a pious hope which needs to be challenged?

- *Size and structure.* How large is the organisation compared to other companies inside and outside the industry? How much 'clout' does it have? Is it a single, simple structure or a complex conglomerate? Is it hierarchical or flat, and restructured or re-engineered? Does it operate in one or several countries? What is the structure of the public relations operation given these factors? Is it an appropriate structure? Should consultancies be used or should everything be handled in-house?

- *Nature of the business.* What activities does the organisation perform? Is it single or multi-product? Does it operate in a single sector or several sectors? Are specialist public relations roles needed, for example is a hi-tech or construction division needed, or can all activities be served from a unified or devolved public relations department?

- *Tradition and history.* Is the company old and established or is it new with its position to establish? Is it well known for doing things in certain ways or is it an unknown quantity? Closely linked to this is the philosophy and culture of the organisation. Is it open and participative or is it hierarchical and directive?

- *Image history.* How has the organisation been perceived over the years? Is it market leading, innovative, reliable, plodding and slow, or slightly shifty? Has the image been constant or has it been subject to rapid or developmental change?

- *Types of employees.* White collar? Blue collar? Graduate? Semi or unskilled? A complete mixture?

All these organisational factors profoundly affect how the public relations function is structured, and how and what the activities are that need to be carried out.

Issues

It is obvious that the issues affecting the society or an industry in which an organisation operates, as well as the specific issues that the organisation faces, are likely to set an agenda for much of the public relations work. Issues generally fall into a number of categories, as follows:

- *Structural.* The major long-term trends in society, such as an ageing population, technological developments, things over which the individual organisation will have very little control.

- *External.* Largely contextual issues such as environmental concerns, community concerns, political imperatives.

- *Crises.* Normally short term and arising from unforeseen events, for example a factory disaster, war, product recall.

- *Internal.* Long or short-term issues that are facing the company from within, for example succession policy and industrial relations.

- *Current affairs.* Those things that are of immediate public interest and which often are the subject of intense media coverage at the time, for example, dangerous dogs legislation following a series of dog attacks reported in the media.

- *Potential.* Those issues that have not yet emerged. It might seem rather odd to list this, but it is very much the case that some issues do appear to arise from nowhere, except that the careful practitioner will have an intelligence system at their disposal that can give early warning of potential issues that are likely to become real. Content analysis of the media can often give an indicator.

Public opinion

Public opinion, often expressed through the media, or even encouraged by the media, is a very potent influence on organisations. The long-running campaign against Barclays Bank eventually led to that company's withdrawal from South Africa. The current campaign against the other major clearing banks, Lloyds, Midland and National Westminster, for their involvement in Third World debt is making things uncomfortable for them and, because of student boycotts, affecting their business.

The media as a reflector of public opinion is vital to public relations because the same channel is used to put across public relations messages. The media often define and crystallise the public mood, although sometimes its influence can be overestimated.

It is certainly true that the media can fatally damage the reputation of an organisation or individual. Sometimes this is because the organisation is genuinely at fault, in which case the media is doing its job of serving the public interest. Sometimes, as libel cases attest, there is little ground for their attacks.

It is also the case that the media can massively enhance the reputation of an organisation by offering free publicity for the good work that it is doing or by favourably reporting on its business performance. This is especially true if comment is made in influential media such as the *Financial Times* if a financial matter is being reported, or in the tabloids and relevant consumer press if a consumer product is being promoted.

Timescales

Obviously timescales are critical when determining public relations programmes. Sometimes the practitioner has the luxury of planning a programme over a self-selected period of time. The reality often is, however, that either external or internal restraints, or both, determine when activities can be performed.

- *Externally driven timescales.* Quite frequently external factors determine when public relations activities take place. If, for example, an organisation wants to change a clause in some proposed legislation, they have to undertake their lobbying within the time frame laid down by Parliament. Other factors such as the announcement of financial results are regulated by the Stock Exchange rules. Information regarding competitive activity may lead to pre-emptive action within very precise time limits.

- *Internally driven timescales.* Examples of internally imposed deadlines are the introduction of a new product, the arrival of a new chief executive, a decision to build a new production line, achievement of an international quality standard and so on.

Resources

The level of resources put into a public relations function or department clearly determine the level and scope of activities that can be undertaken. The resourcing of specific programmes is discussed in Chapter 8. However, it is appropriate here to cover it briefly.

Normally there are two approaches. The first is to determine an appropriate departmental structure along with the relevant activities that need to be undertaken, and to provide the human and financial resources to carry them out.

The second approach is to devote to public relations a budget, broadly in line with the resourcing also given to other departments in the organisation. For example, 10 per cent of the overall marketing budget is a figure sometimes quoted. The trick then is to prioritise the public relations activities and to carry out those essential elements of the programme within budget.

What is absolutely guaranteed is that the ideal budget will always be considerably more than that allocated! But that's life and public relations practitioners like everyone else have to live within their budgets.

While the other six areas give an overall context to public relations, it is true to say that timescales and resources are constraining factors on activity.

Organising for action

The way the public relations operation is usually organised is to split it along either task or functional lines. Single operators, however, have to do everything!

Some organisations have a task-oriented structure, that is, the individual jobs or tasks are separated out and given to small groups or individuals to perform. Thus the structure may be as follows:

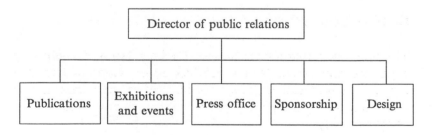

Other organisations split on functional lines. That is the areas of activity are separated out and groups or individuals tackle all the tasks. A functional structure may look something like this:

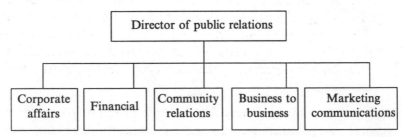

Where public relations is conducted for a company that is split into separate operating companies, sometimes with different names, the situation is infinitely more variable. Some groups have very large corporate departments which undertake activity for the group as a whole and for all the operating companies. In other groups there is a very small corporate operation dealing with major corporate activities such as financial and government affairs, and maybe corporate sponsorship. The rest of the activity is then devolved out to the operating companies. Normally the operating pattern that applies in the business as a whole also applies to public relations activity, that is, if business is very much controlled from the centre then public relations is likely to be controlled from the centre also. On the other hand, if the approach is to let the operating companies function as virtually autonomous units, then that is also likely to be the approach for public relations.

Who does what in public relations?

In their seminal work on public relations James Grunig and Todd Hunt[1] refer to work spearheaded by Glen Broom and

---

[1] Grunig, J E and Hunt, T (1992) *Managing Public Relations*, Holt, Rinehart and Winston, 2nd edn.

David Dozier in which two dominant public relations roles were identified.

- *The communication technician.* Who is not involved in making organisational decisions, but who carries out public relations programmes such as writing press releases, editing house magazines and producing videos. This person is probably not too involved in undertaking research or evaluating programmes; they are concerned primarily with implementation.

- *The communication manager.* Who plans and manages public relations programmes, counsels management, makes communication policy decisions and so on.

Within this second category, there are three main types of manager role.

- *The expert prescriber.* Who researches and defines public relations problems, develops programmes and implements them, maybe with the assistance of others.

- *The communication facilitator.* Who acts as a go-between, keeping two-way communication between an organisation and its publics. They are a liaison person, interpreter and mediator.

- *The problem-solving process facilitator.* Who helps others in the organisation solve their public relations problems. This person acts as a sort of counsellor/adviser on the planning and implementation of programmes. (This is a role often fulfilled by specialist consultancies.)

David Dozier also identifies two middle level roles that sit between the manager and technician role.

- *Media relations role.* This is a two-way function where the individual keeps the media informed, and informs the organisation of the needs and concerns of the media. This is not just the production and dissemination of messages from the organisation to the media, but a highly skilled role requiring detailed knowledge and a profound understanding of the media. This role is often fulfilled by someone who has made the crossover from journalism to public relations. It also goes some way to explaining why, if a former journalist is employed to undertake public relations, the function remains focused on media relations.

- *Communication and liaison role.* Serves higher level public relations managers by representing the organisation at events and meetings, and positively creating opportunities for management to communicate with internal and external publics.

The broad technician and manager roles vary from organisation to organisation. At the lower level, in large organisations split on task lines, a technician may only write for the house journal. In other organisations they may do several other writing jobs too, especially if the department is functional in orientation or if it is small.

At the middle level, practitioners may be responsible for a whole press relations programme or undertake employee relations only. They may be involved in both. Some may specialise in research or planning and have little to do with implementation, or they may be an account executive in a consultancy who has to turn their hand to a whole range of planning and implementation tasks.

At higher levels, public relations managers plan whole programmes and counsel senior management on policy, as well as supervise middle and lower level practitioners.

In practice most public relations activities require a mixture of technician and manager roles. Many managers hold a number of the management roles indicated either at the same time, or at various stages in their careers, and not many people, at this stage of the profession's growth, are entirely removed from the implementation role.

The growing complexity of the issues that public relations practitioners are being asked to handle is leading to increasing specialisation in some areas. At the simplest level this is demonstrated by the fact that many consultancies now bill themselves as specialists in, for example, fashion or personality or hi-tech public relations and the larger, one-stop agencies have for a long time had quite discrete specialist functions within them, such as public affairs or consumer divisions.

3

Starting the planning process

Getting in control

Having looked at public relations within the business context and recognising the various factors that affect how public relations is structured and conducted, we can now look at the planning process itself.

Public relations practitioners are very busy individuals. First of all they have operational responsibilities like anyone else who works in a disciplined environment. If they hold a management role they have to handle budgets and people, run an effective department or consultancy, control suppliers, ensure quality standards are met and so on. In fact all the skills required of any manager are required of public relations professionals.

There are also other pressures. Much of the work is high profile. A mistake made when talking to a journalist has very public consequences. In fact, most of the activities of public relations professionals is by definition 'public'. It's a profession where there are very few ground rules: the practice is not highly prescribed as it is for other professions. Often the role is not properly understood by colleagues. The work is usually under-taken under deadline and there is always too much to do. There are severe qualitative and quantitative pressures on practitioners.

The public relations brief is a large one: to manage the communication interface between the organisation and all its publics. That is a very tall order.

To succeed, a systematic, efficient approach to the job in hand is essential. As far as possible you need to be in control, although total control in the dynamic world of communication is impossible and not even desirable.

Public relations policy

The first requirement is for a clear public relations policy to be laid down. This should define the remit of public relations activity and set the ground rules for operation.

The idea of a policy is not to be regulatory and restrictive, but to give the rules of engagement so that everyone knows where responsibility lies, where the lines of demarcation are and, ultimately, who is accountable for what activities.

Policy statements need not be long or complicated, but they must be clear.

Figure 3.1 shows an example from Pilkington PLC of its corporate public relations policy. Pilkington has a group (corporate) public relations function which deals largely with company-wide matters and which agreed this policy with senior management. It also has several divisions and subsidiaries that have their own public relations activities.

CORPORATE PUBLIC RELATIONS POLICY

1. Meetings with the city press must be kept at a level consistent with maintaining satisfactory relationships and will be arranged through Group Public Relations.

   Statements to the city press may be made only by General Board directors, or by Group Public Relations acting on the Board's instructions.

2. The Group will not normally publicise through the media its attitudes to matters that are politically sensitive at local or national level. Considerable time is expended by directors and some senior managers on representing the company's interests to legislators, parliamentarians, and others with the ability to affect the company's future; these contacts can be prejudiced by inopportune publicity.

3. The Group will not offer public comment on the wisdom or otherwise of budgetary or other legislative measures. It may be prepared to give factual evidence about the effects of such measures on the performance of any part of the Group when such effects can be demonstrated.

4. Public comment, in the press or elsewhere, must relate to historic or current activities. Comment about future plans and/or prospects must be avoided so far as is practicable.

5. Announcements about possible or planned capital invest-ments or disinvestments may not normally be made until such projects have been formally authorised by the General Board.

   Where local or national government agencies need to be consulted in advance of an investment, it may be necessary to make an earlier announcement. In such cases, the limited extent of the commitment at that stage must be emphasised. Dates for starting or completing projects must be given in a form that will allow for contingencies.

6. No announcements should be made about negotiations, eg. licensing agreements, co-operative agreements with other companies, until negotiations are successfully completed and

the form of announcement has been agreed by the parties concerned.

7. Opportunities for favourable publicity will be identified by Group Public Relations and exploited after clearance at Executive Director level.

8. Divisions, subsidiaries and functions retaining external public relations advisers in whatever capacity should ensure that the constraints of their role are very clearly defined, if necessary in consultation with Group Public Relations.

   Under no circumstances must retained advisers be permitted to make public statements on behalf of Pilkington, or to lobby on behalf of Pilkington, without prior clearance through Group Public Relations.

9. Where circumstances suggest that action should be taken which would be at variance with these guidelines, such action should not be taken without prior clearance from the Chairman or a Deputy Chairman, with the involvement of Group Public Relations.

10. Divisions, subsidiaries and functions should ensure that Group Public Relations are briefed and consulted on all occasions where these guidelines have a relevance.

    These guidelines are not intended to restrict divisional public relations activities in the marketing area where there is established liaison with Group Public Relations.

Figure 3.1. *Pilkington PLC corporate public relations policy*

Once the areas of operation have been confirmed, activities need to be planned and managed.

Why planning is important

It is quite legitimate to ask 'Why plan'? There is always so much to do, why not just get on and do it?

Apart from the vital fact of putting you in control, as discussed in Chapter 1, there are several other good reasons for planning.

- *It focuses effort.* It ensures the unnecessary is excluded. It makes you work on the right things. It helps you to work smart instead of just working hard. It enables you to operate efficiently and effectively because you are concentrating on the priorities.

- *It improves effectiveness.* By working on the right things, defined objectives will be achieved. Time and money will be saved because effort isn't being diverted into worthy, but less important tasks. Importantly it makes saying 'No' to unplanned things much easier. Or at least you can say, 'If I take on this task, which of my other prioritised jobs should I drop?' In other words planning to objectives gives you a benchmark for measurement.

- *Encourages the long-term view.* By definition, to plan you have to look ahead. This forces you to take a longer perspective than the immediate here and now. It forces you to look around at the organisation and its priorities and at the broader business context, and helps you to produce a structured programme to meet future as well as current needs.

- *Helps demonstrate value for money.* This is applicable whether working in-house or in consultancy. If there is a fight for budgets, then demonstrating past achievements and being able to present a powerful, costed programme gives you a point from which to argue your case for money.

- *Minimises mishaps.* Careful planning means that at the macro level different scenarios have been considered and the most appropriate selected. It means that there is meticulous contingency planning and all the angles have been covered. At the micro level, planning makes day-to-day work tolerable, even fun.

- *Reconciles conflicts.* When putting together a programme or a campaign there are always conflicts of interests and priorities. Planning helps you confront those difficulties before they arise and helps you work them through to resolution.

- *Facilitates proactivity.* Setting your own agenda is vitally important. Of course public relations work is about reacting to media demands or responding quickly to a crisis, but it is also about deciding what *you* want to do; what actions *you* want to take, what messages *you* want to put across. Planning a comprehensive and cohesive programme helps you achieve this.

Planning applies to everything, whether it is to complete programmes and campaigns lasting one or five years or even longer, or to individual activities such as a press conference or the briefing of suppliers.

Basic questions in planning

The planning process is really quite simple. The trick is to break things down into a manageable sequence. It is helpful to ask five basic questions.

What do I want to achieve?	(What are my objectives?)
Who do I want to talk to?	(Who are my publics?)
What do I want to say?	(What are the messages I want to get across?)
How shall I say it?	(What mechanisms shall I use to get my messages across?)

How do I know I've got it   (How will I evaluate my work)
right?

And the purpose of the activity is to influence behaviour in some way.

In order to answer these questions there are two major requirements.

- *Information.* Finding out everything there is to know about the task in hand – careful research and analysis.
- *Strategy.* Using that information to identify the guiding principles and main thrust of the programme.

From these two requirements comes the tactical programme which can be evaluated for effectiveness.

At this stage it should be noted that the list of questions includes questions about information-seeking and research (objectives, publics, messages and evaluation), but only one question about the actual doing.

This is about the right proportion of effort that should go into the planning process. Get the research and analysis right, and the programme should then virtually write itself. Please note, it is not being suggested that 80 per cent of the time spent on a programme should be put into information seeking. That is plainly wrong as you would never get anything done. However, 80 per cent of the planning effort to devise an appropriate programme is put into research. Once having put all that work into planning, the implementation should run smoothly and effectively.

The ten stages of planning

To expand on the above, we can now look at a sequence of planning steps that will ensure an effective programme (long-term overall programme with long-term objectives) or campaign (individual campaign with very specific short-term objectives) is put together:

- analysis;
- objectives;
- publics (audiences);
- messages;
- strategy;
- tactics;
- timescales;
- resources;
- evaluation;
- review.

Sometimes the analysis and objectives are in reverse order. An organisation might give its public relations department or consultancy a list of objectives they want them to achieve. However, these objectives must be carefully scrutinised in order to see if they are appropriate. For example, the organisation may say they have a problem recruiting good new staff. After careful analysis, the public relations professionals may discover that the real problem is not recruitment, but retention of good staff, thus the objectives of the programme will have to change and an internal rather than external campaign will have to be mounted which addresses employment policies as well as communication issues.

The planning process is illustrated in Figure 3.2.

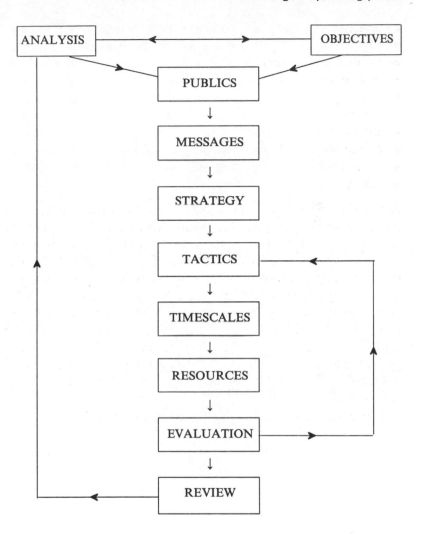

Figure 3.2 *The planning process in logical steps*

The planning process looks quite straightforward when laid out like this. However, there are often problems in practice. Sometimes there is a lack of detailed information on which to base the plan. This may be because senior managers are not prepared to share the wider game-plan, or it may be that a client only wants to give a consultancy limited information for reasons of confidentiality. Perhaps the campaign itself is very complex or fast moving, for example a complicated takeover bid. It could be that the plan is being executed under extreme time pressure, even in a crisis. It is often the case that the resources devoted to programmes are less than ideal and so corners have to be cut or the programme pruned. There also is the possibility that there are conflicting priorities arising part-way through the programme that require energy and resources to be diverted from the original course of action.

The planning scheme outlined does give a solid basis for planning and the pattern can be followed whatever the scale of the task. If the programme is particularly large it may be necessary to split it down into a series of projects which follow the same steps. Thus you might have a public affairs programme and a community relations programme, each with focused objectives and restricted publics, which feed into an overall programme with wider objectives and broader publics and messages. This is illustrated in Figure 3.3.

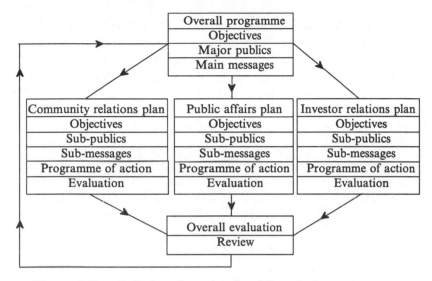

Figure 3.3. *Splitting the overall public relations programme into manageable sub-sections*

Of course it goes without saying that planning is an aid to effective working and not an end in itself. It is not meant to be a straitjacket. We live in a complex and changing environment where flexibility and adaptability are essential. We all know the kind of person who says that because something has not been planned it cannot be done. In public relations, of all disciplines, there has to be a capability to react and adjust to the dynamic organisational and communications environment in which we operate. Sometimes objectives and tactics have to change – rapidly. That's life in public relations.

Plans are made to ensure that we focus on what's necessary and achieve what we are meant to. Once laid down, they are not in tablets of stone – realism is everything. However the planning process holds good, even if programmes have to be adjusted, and the steps given in Figure 3.2 are valid whatever changes are needed.

4

Analysis

The first planning step

Analysis is the first part of the planning process. This entails research in order to identify the issues on which to base your public relations programme. Without getting to the core issues you will not have a credible or effective programme, or one that addresses corporate objectives.

If the core issue is that your products are regarded as old fashioned and therefore you are losing market share, your programme will have to be about demonstrating that your products are modern and leading edge (providing that they are), not that they are cheaper than those of your competitors!

There isn't room in this book to look at the whole area of research in public relations. Complete volumes have been written on the subject. However, it is possible to give an overview.

When starting a programme from scratch it is vital that the basic ground research on the overall context of the public relations function is undertaken (see Chapter 2). It is vitally important to look at not only the micro environment and the immediate things that affect the organisation, but also the macro environment.

A commonly used and immensely valuable technique is a PEST analysis. PEST divides the overall environment into four areas and covers just about everything that can affect an organisation. The four areas are: Political, Economic, Social and Technological.

The main questions to ask when undertaking a PEST analysis are as follows.

- What are the environmental factors that affect the organisation?
- Which of these are currently most important?
- Which will be most important in the next four years?

The grid below gives some headings that should be considered under the four areas.

POLITICAL	ECONOMIC
Environmental legislation	Interest rates
Employment legislation	Inflation
Trade (including overseas) legislation	Money supply
Change/continuance of government	Levels of employment
	Disposable income
	Business/economic cycles
	World business/economic conditions
	Energy costs
SOCIAL	TECHNOLOGICAL
Population shifts and growth	New discoveries
Lifestyles	Rate of change
Levels of education	Investment in technology
Income/wealth distribution	Spending on research and development
Consumer patterns	Obsolescence
Social attitudes and concerns	

Having generated a list of possible environmental influences, the main ones have to be identified. So, for example, someone working in the higher educational field in the western world will have to consider the following three key factors. The first is to do with demographics; the proportion of people under 21 is decreasing so the higher education system will have to adapt itself to teaching a higher proportion of mature students. The second is that the use of technology in teaching is transforming the traditional teacher/student relationship. Third, the requirement for a higher proportion of the population to have at least first degree level qualifications or their equivalent means there will be more students in the higher education system demanding resources, yet those resources are critically dependent on the economic state of individual countries and the priorities that governments put on education.

PEST analysis also helps to identify the long-term drivers of change. For example, some markets are becoming more global and it is vital to identify the factors involved in that, such as the use of technology. The worldwide similarity of consumer tastes in some areas such as soft drinks, electronic goods and sport leads to opportunities for global approaches to marketing and manufacturing.

The PEST analysis process also can identify how external influences can affect organisations in different ways. So a company that traditionally sources its raw materials from a number of countries is less likely to be vulnerable to a political crisis than a company that sources its raw materials from a single, cheaper supplier in a country with a less stable political regime.

Some organisations are more affected by one of the four PEST areas than others. For example, the political context is vitally important to local government, whereas economic factors may be more important to retailing organisations.

It is interesting to note how this kind of analysis matches classic strategic business planning as demonstrated in Figure 4.1.

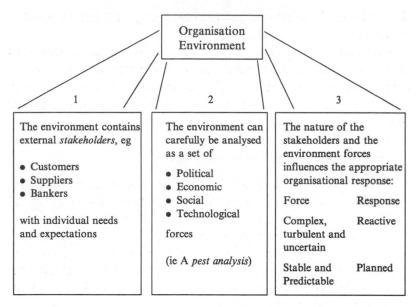

Figure 4.1. *Analysis of Organisation Environment undertaken in strategic planning*[1]

The difference is that for public relations the focus will be on communications issues.

Spotting the issues

By carrying out a thorough-going PEST analysis which looks not only at current but also future developments, it is possible to identify the most significant issues that might affect the organisation and to track those issues. A number of the media monitoring companies now offer an issues analysis service. They track not only what are the most prevalent issues of the day overall (for example, views on current economic performance), but they also spot those issues that are beginning to appear on

---

[1] Thompson, J L (1995) *Strategy in Action*, Chapman Hall.

the agenda because they are beginning to attract media coverage.

Forward looking companies spend a great deal of time and effort on issues management. They constantly scan the wider environment to determine which issues they should be paying particular regard to. Issues that are not identified or not taken seriously have a nasty habit of coming back to haunt you as crises.

Issues management works in two ways.

- It identifies those issues over which the organisation can have no control, where public opinion is inevitably going to move in a particular direction and therefore it would be foolish for the company to maintain or take up a position that flies in the face of the prevailing view. It would be very odd if an organisation in the west were to promulgate the view that large families are to be encouraged when a major concern is over-population.

  In this situation an organisation has to examine its policies and practices, and bring them into line with public opinion, or it risks losing the sympathy and support of its stakeholders.

  Organisations that are adept at issues management not only handle current issues, but also predict the likely public reaction to emerging concerns and position themselves as leaders by changing their policies and practices or adopting new ones ahead of anyone else. They can be seen to be leading the field rather than being forced to react because of prevailing opinion. They do this not just to get ahead, but because they are progressive, ethical and responsive to the likely demands of their stakeholders.

- It detects those issues where the organisation can have an input into the emerging debate and therefore shape its outcome in an ethical and beneficial way. An example of this is Rhone-Poulenc Agriculture's ten-year experiment looking at organic versus conventional farming (ie farming with agro-chemicals), which is trying to determine the best farming method, economically, environmentally and in food quality terms. By establishing the facts about both systems the company will be able to make a definitive contribution to the debate. It will also be bound by the results, whatever they are.

Thus issues analysis works in both directions: detecting those external factors, political, economic, social or technological that require the company to change; and identifying those areas where it might have an input into the public debate and influence the outcome.

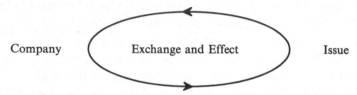

Company   Exchange and Effect   Issue

Any comprehensive public relations programme must address long-term issues. Individual public relations campaigns must also identify any relevant issues which, depending on the nature of the campaign, may be long or short term. Obviously a campaign to launch an individual car care product will not require such a wide-ranging examination of the issues as a five-year programme to relaunch and reposition a charity.

In summary it is important to know the broad organisational context, the organisation itself, the issues affecting the organisation, the mood of public opinion, and the views and aspirations of stakeholders (groups of individuals who can influence the performance of an organisation, for example employees, cus-tomers and suppliers – more on this in Chapter 6.)

Having analysed the broader environmental context it is necessary to apply these specifically to the organisation.

SWOT Analysis

One way to approach this is to divide these considerations by SWOT analysis. The first two elements, Strengths and Weaknesses, can be seen as internally driven and particular to the organisation. The other two, Opportunities and Threats, are normally external and will have been largely identified through the PEST analysis. The four elements can be seen as mirror segments in a quadrant. Below is a brief example.

STRENGTHS	WEAKNESSES
Financially strong	Conservative in investment
Innovative	Restricted product line
Good leadership	Traditional and hierarchical
Good reputation	Only really known for one product
Loyal workforce	Inflexible working patterns
OPPORTUNITIES	THREATS
Cheap supplies from Eastern Europe	Instability of Eastern bloc
To expand into China	Uncertainty over Hong Kong
To acquire competitors	To be taken over by conglomerate

It is sometimes useful to list the elements of the SWOT analysis into categories, for example corporate, product, internal and so on.

Taking the above analysis into consideration we can see that our public relations programme will have a number of jobs to do in support of corporate objectives. For example, we will need to mount a marketing communications campaign if our product line is to be expanded. We will want an internal communications programme to assist in managing change. An international corporate and government relations campaign will be required if we are to expand into China, and we will certainly need a financial relations programme if we are to preserve our strong reputation, raise capital to fund expansion and offset takeover possibilities.

What State the Stakeholder

Having determined what the key issues are and the organisation's stance on them, it is then the public relations professional's job to communicate with and receive feedback from the various stakeholders.

Before doing that, however, the state of the relationship between the organisation and its stakeholders also needs analysis. If the view that stakeholders have of an organisation differs from the actual facts of the case, there is a further issue that needs to be addressed. The problem may be lack of information, or wrong information, that can be countered quite easily. The problem might be more profound or complex, for example the organisation might have a reputation for being a bad employer because it had to make 50 per cent of its workforce redundant to survive several years before and the legacy lingers on.

You then have to discover if a real communications problem exists, what the actual problem is, with whom (which stakeholders) what messages need to be communicated, how they should be communicated and whether or not they are effective.

To get the necessary answers research is required or, as Roger Haywood[1] in his book *All About Public Relations* puts it – 'intelligence' – that is assimilated and interpreted information. It is impossible to change attitudes or behaviour without knowing what the starting point is.

It is worth saying that research shouldn't just be done when a programme is being planned. It should be an on-going process. It should be used to monitor the progress of a programme or campaign and it should certainly be used to evaluate effectiveness once a campaign has ended.

The number of times a complete review of an organisation and its communication takes place is quite rare. It usually happens when the public relations function is just established, when a new head is appointed or if there is a strategic review. Consultancies, when pitching for business, will, as part of their background research, undertake this kind of analysis to a greater or lesser extent.

However, most practitioners are involved in planning annual programmes or campaigns and the same basic disciplines apply. Research around the topic in hand needs to be rigorous and

---

[1] Haywood, R (1991) *All About Public Relations*, McGraw-Hill, 2nd edn.

objective, but it need not necessarily be expensive – it depends on the task. If you want to find out the views of the local community, it is a simple matter to walk the streets and ask, to go to the local pubs, to ask the local Rotary or Lions clubs and to speak to local community leaders. This might be all that is required. If, however, you want to launch a major campaign aimed at changing the country's eating habits, much more detailed and sophisticated research will be required.

The principles behind doing research are the same whether they are for major, strategic, long-term programmes or short campaigns. Research helps you establish what the nature and style of the communication task is, what the objectives should be, what publics should be addressed, what messages and methods should be employed, and whether or not you have succeeded in your objectives.

Sometimes the communication task seems obvious, but research doesn't just tell you what you need to communicate. A company may want to fight proposed legislation that threatens a large part of its business. Research will reveal the size of the task, the best way to tackle it (messages and mechanisms) and also indicate the chances of success – there is no point in spending money on lost causes.

Who should undertake the research?

Given that whole programmes or campaigns are based on research, it is important that it is carried out properly. It is not good enough to instruct the most junior member of the public relations team to contact a few customers to find out what they think of the existing corporate identity. Those involved in serious research must be properly trained. There is no point in spending a lot of money getting biased or incomplete answers. There are several excellent short courses and text books on conducting research. You don't have to spend a fortune to become competent at collecting basic information and interpreting it properly.

Obviously if you employ an established research consultancy or use trained in-house people they will know all about undertaking statistically valid research which involves selecting a sample that genuinely reflects the universe being studied.

Sometimes it is entirely legitimate to do a 'quick and dirty' study of, for example, reactions of personal finance journalists to a new pension plan, as long as you recognise the limitations of that study and don't try to use it as anything other than a fairly superficial survey of a very particular group of people.

The benefits of using trained in-house researchers are that they know the business and will need little briefing except for the specifics of the research problem. On the downside, they may be seen to be less objective than external researchers and there is always the syndrome of the prophet honoured everywhere but in his own country to contend with.

External researchers could very well offer specialist skills in specialised research areas, including communication. They may be perceived to be more objective, but are often (although not necessarily) more expensive because they build in learning time, overheads, profits and so on.

Of course, it is perfectly possible to mix the two. You could get professional advice on questionnaire design, administer it yourself and get a research company to analyse the results for you.

Research techniques

There are several different types of research. First of all there is quantitative research which collects data that is then expressed statistically giving results in numbers or quantities, and there is qualitative research which investigates non-quantifiable variables such as opinions, reactions and attitudes. Thus, measuring how many people will vote for a particular party at a general election is quantitative research; finding out what views an individual has on the policies of the major political parties is qualitative research.

Continuous or tracking research is where the same group of people or people of the same profile are asked the same questions at regular intervals. Television companies often have a panel of viewers whom they will contact regularly to find out what they have viewed and what their opinions are of various programmes. Building societies regularly survey groups of people on a one-off basis, but with the same characteristics, to find out what awareness of the various societies is. The large research companies frequently survey business people to discover all kinds of things from their views on the economy to opinions on executive pay.

Surveys have been undertaken on just about anything from how many people with blue eyes like baked beans to what people thought of France's performance in the last football world cup.

Continuous or tracking surveys are particularly helpful when trying to measure something like consumer trends or changes in attitude over time. One-off surveys are useful if you need some definitive factual information on which to base a campaign. For example, you will want to know what proportion of the population buys wigs before you launch a new kind of wig.

Then there is primary and secondary research. Secondary research is often called desk research and entails collecting information from already published sources. There is an enormous amount of published data that can be accessed. The trick is knowing where to find it. Public and university libraries have vast collections of material on companies and industry sectors, social trends and so on. They are often connected to international information databases. They also have newspapers and magazines archived on databases and CD ROM, as do trade libraries run by professional bodies such as the Law Society. Government departments hold statistics on subjects relevant to them. Company reports and corporate and product literature are available from most organisations. Almost everything under the sun has been surveyed at some stage and most libraries are happy to point you in the right direction if you ask nicely. The Internet also provides huge possibilities for obtaining information from individuals and organisations worldwide.

The large research companies such as Mintel, MORI and Gallup conduct their own surveys on various topics, and you can ask for a listing and buy their reports very easily. Of course desk research takes time and hiring the services of a professional researcher could make the task much easier if time means money to you. However research that has already been conducted is often a great deal cheaper than doing the work yourself. A quick call and a small fee to a research organisation to find out what's available could save you a great deal of money.

Primary research is finding out the information you want at first hand. There are various techniques for obtaining primary data.

Self-completion questionnaires

These are a relatively cheap way to contact a large number of people over a geographically widespread area (or even a small number of people in a geographically tight area). They are excellent for obtaining information from people who are difficult to contact (maybe they are shift workers) and they allow time for people to consider their answers carefully before responding. It is useful to include an incentive (for example, free entry to a prize draw) to encourage a good response. Self-completion questionnaires need to be clear, simple and as short as possible. They can be distributed and collected by post, in person or via another medium such as a magazine and are usually completed by the respondent without supervision. If a questionnaire is more complex they can be issued to groups with a trained researcher supervising the session or answering questions which may arise.

Questionnaires are often used to obtain a mass of quantitative data, but can also be used for qualitative material. Good questionnaires that are unbiased, unambiguous and which collect all the information that is required are very difficult to design. Professional help must often be sought from trained researchers.

One-to-one interviews

This survey technique is excellent for collecting qualitative data. Interviews are obviously time consuming for the researcher and the interviewee, and this method is very expensive if a mass of data is required. There are ways in which you can keep the cost of interviewing down. It is relatively cheap to participate in an omnibus survey which may be run by one of the larger research organisations. They often undertake regular surveys on specific groups such as teenagers and industry sectors like motoring, and on particular products such as computer games. You can add a few questions to the survey and you are charged per question. Results from these interviews can usually be turned around very quickly, often within a few days.

There are also syndicated studies where the results are available to those who subscribe to the service. The survey mentioned earlier where building societies track awareness is a syndicated study with the participating building societies obtaining the results for a fee.

Although relatively expensive, the quality and quantity of information that can be gathered from tailor-made one-to-one interviews can be superb. Again it is important to stress that interviewing is a particular skill and training is required to get the best from the opportunity. Interviews can be structured so that specific information is collected, unstructured where the questions are developed as a result of the answers given, or somewhere in between – semi-structured.

Interviewing allows the researcher to explore views and opinions in depth, and the reasons why those views are held. When trying to get to the heart of difficult issues it is an excellent technique to use. Sophisticated computer programs are now available to analyse text, picking out key words and phrases, and facilitate quantitative as well as qualitative analysis.

Telephone interviews

This is an increasingly popular technique, particularly suitable for collecting structured information. They are a kind of halfway house between face-to-face interviews and question-naires. They don't allow as much probing as the face-to-face interview or the reflection of the questionnaire, but they are a relatively speedy way to collect information from a broad or narrow section of respondents. The Computer Aided Telephone Interview (CATI) system allows researchers to input answers to questions very quickly and instant analysis is possible. CATI systems also provide call management facilities such as organising calls, redialing engaged numbers and keeping statistics of failed contacts.

Focus groups

Focus groups are discussion groups comprising carefully selected individuals (maybe with the same profile, for example 20 to 25-year-old Asian women, married with children, all born in the UK and living in Cardiff; or maybe with very different backgrounds). Running a successful focus group is a very skilled activity and requires a highly competent co-ordinator to guide discussion and to ensure all the relevant questions are asked. The idea behind a focus group is that the responses from the participants prompt and develop responses from other partici-pants. Properly done, focus groups can obtain far more information than one-to-one interviews. There are difficulties associated with this technique: selection of participants, length of time needed, facilities required (room, recording equipment), expense (travel costs, refreshments), but the depth of insight that can be acquired is a rich reward.

Informal research

Apart from the formal research techniques, there are all kinds of ways of obtaining information about issues and organisations. Chance encounters and informal discussions with the whole range of publics associated with an organisation such as competitors, specialist journalists, neighbours and suppliers can be very enlightening. Getting a feel for the organisation by attending its annual general meeting or social events helps. Don't just talk to the self-important people: cleaners, secretaries and security people are important too, and are often more honest and realistic. Regular reading of the quality press, listening to and watching general interest and current affairs programmes, even discussions with friends and colleagues in social situations, helps to build an all-embracing overview of the context and the specifics of any particular situation, and helps you make connections between issues and organisations that might not be available via formal research.

Informal, or 'quick and dirty' research, should not be discounted either. A very successful campaign to save a London hospital was based on the public relations executive walking the streets surrounding the hospital asking people about it and talking to people in the pub. Oh, and the executive had a lot of experience in public relations! Not a procedure recommended as exemplary, but time was pressing and it worked!

Media research

It is important not only to know your organisation and the relevant issues, but to investigate the channels of communication too. The written and broadcast media provide information on readership profiles, circulation, effectiveness of advertising, reaction to copy and so on. Other media such as direct mail, advertising, posters and sponsorship can also be analysed. The various media have their own trade bodies that can provide all kinds of information on their use and effectiveness, and this should be carefully considered when deciding which channels should be used for particular publics.

Communication audit

Apart from researching the issues affecting an organisation or the facts surrounding a particular campaign it is vitally important for the public relations professional to examine in detail the communication process itself. This is done via a communication audit. In brief a communication audit identifies those publics vital to an organisation's success. It investigates the scope of communication to determine whether all existing or potential publics are being covered. It examines their current attitudes and assesses whether or not work is required to crystallise, confirm or adjust those attitudes. It appraises critically the nature and quality of the communication between the organisation and its publics, looking carefully at the messages that are being relayed to see if they are what is required, their frequency and the techniques that are used to transmit them, as well as the effectiveness of the communication. It identifies communication gaps and unexploited opportunities, as well as the information needs of all the key publics. It also looks ahead by examining future information requirements and new methods of communication that should be used. An audit also pinpoints the resources and skills needed to run a successful programme or campaign, and whether or not these are available to an organisation.

To undertake an effective audit requires extensive research both within an organisation, with the whole range of personnel responsible for communication, and outside an organisation to investigate the opinions of those who are in contact with it.

Interpreting the findings

Collecting data is all very well and can be fun! But what do you do with all this data once you have it? At the risk of becoming boring it is important to stress that analysing and interpreting data is a skilled job. All too often very simple analysis is done on very rich data. Obvious conclusions are drawn from simple statistics. It could be that 24 per cent of your sample said no to your question, 26 per cent said yes, but 50 per cent said maybe. What does that mean? It could well be that enlightenment will come from using information from other parts of the survey. The golden rule is: once having paid good money for research, milk it for all it's worth, and you might need a professional to help you do that.

Exploitation of research in the public relations context

A great deal of your research will be done to enable you to focus your public relations effort more effectively. Identifying what the real issues of concern are for your various stakeholders means that you can concentrate your efforts on those. Establishing just what the attitudes of your stakeholders are will indicate how large the communications task is if you are trying to achieve a shift in those attitudes. This research, although vital, provides you mainly with essential background information.

However, research can be used much more overtly within programmes and campaigns. You come up front and say you have specifically researched certain topics. You may well add extra credibility by enlisting the services of one of the more well-known and respected research agencies to undertake the work for you. Indeed one of the more sure-fire media 'hooks' is to base a media campaign on research. The magical words are 'A survey has revealed'!

The best way to illustrate how research can be exploited in public relations campaigns is to give a good example.

Britain's undiscovered billions: A Lansons Communications campaign for IFA Promotion Limited, the organisation representing Britain's independent financial advisers.

In 1993 Lansons began a new campaign-led approach to IFA Promotion's marketing strategy. A year-long campaign called Tax Action focused on the £8 billion we pay every year in unnecessary tax. The solution was for people to use Independent Financial Advisers (IFAs) to get the correct professional financial advice. IFA Promotion ran a consumer hotline which gave callers the names of their three nearest IFAs. The campaign was a great success and responses to the hotline increased by 160 per cent.

The task in 1994 was to build upon the success of the previous year, to convince more ABC1s to use professional advisers and contact the hotline. Promoting independent financial advice was the preferred route and convincing IFAs to run marketing initiatives based on IFA Promotion's lead was an ongoing objective.

The new campaign was designed to keep the best of Tax Action and broaden its appeal. It also aimed to add to the theme. 'Britain's Undiscovered Billions' looked at all the money wasted each year through financial mismanagement or inertia. Two new types of waste apart from tax were highlighted: 'dead money', the focus being missed return because money not needed day-to-day is left idle (often in current accounts); and 'buried treasure', money that is rightfully ours, but left unclaimed, from for example, legacies, premium bonds and state benefits.

The underpinning of Undiscovered Billions was research done by Mintel who quantified the waste. The research was based on an analysis of the Inland Revenue's own 'Personal Income Survey' which gives an in-depth analysis of 70,000 individual cases. Additional data was obtained from the Target Group Index (TGI) survey conducted by the British Market Research Bureau (BMRB) among 25,000 adults each year and other conclusions were based on industry analysis. In this case, no primary research was needed. (You don't necessarily have to leave your desk to undertake first class research.)

What the research discovered was that in 1994, British people could have been £12 billion better off – that's an average of £300 per adult if only we managed our finances better.

Mintel broke the £12 billion into three main areas.

- Over £5 billion paid each year in unnecessary taxation, through allowances not being properly used, lack of proper tax planning and failure to make full use of tax efficient products such as Tax Exempt Special Savings Accounts (TESSAs) and Personal Equity Plans (PEPs).
- Nearly £4 billion came into the 'buried treasure' category.
- Nearly £3 billion could be either earned on the £30 billion 'dead money' that is not working hard enough for us or saved by reducing the £8 billion of unnecessary personal borrowing.

Lansons used the research as a platform both for the media campaign and the local marketing campaign run by IFAs.

The research was launched to the media with a press

conference invitation asking 'How much belongs to your readers?' Robert Kilroy Silk fronted the national press launch with cartoonist Richardson and fashion photographer Charlie Kemp providing excellent visual material. Parallel campaigns ran in the 12 regions examined by the research.

Following the launch, the Mintel figures have been used to launch 12 separate public relations initiatives. These mini campaigns, rolled out at a rate of two per month, have covered topics such as holiday currency and money wasted by not shopping around for insurance.

Lansons also put together a 'case studies' database of people helped by IFAs for use by the press (150 IFAs countrywide co-operated). Video News Release footage based on real-life case studies was also prepared.

An advertorial campaign, run with the Newspaper Society, was taken up by over 100 regional newspapers. In preparation for the consumer campaign the IFAs who wanted to take part in the local marketing push were invited to one of six regional seminars run by IFA Promotion. IFAs were encouraged to focus their own marketing on the Undiscovered Billions theme. To help them, a marketing pack giving details of over 20 ways IFAs could generate income by using the theme was put together. This included shell ads, draft client letters focusing on different aspects of the theme, ideas for seminars, posters, case studies, a comprehensive summary of the Mintel findings and a copy of the Money Detector booklet which was given out free by IFA Promotion when people contacted their hotline.

The results of this research-based campaign were quite exceptional.

In the first five months of the campaign, 46,500 people contacted the IFA Promotion hotline, up by 58 per cent from 1993. Over 40,000 people requested the Money Detector booklet.

IFA Promotion's annual Gallup monitoring survey showed that 56 per cent of ABC1 adults are likely to go to IFAs for advice, should they require it in the future (up from 46 per cent in 1992). Recognition of the blue IFA logo went up from 41 per cent to 52 per cent.

Over 75 per cent of IFA Promotion's 4000 strong membership took part in the Tax Action campaign, 300 attended one of the seminars, 500 attended follow-up seminars and 2000 bought the marketing pack. Hundreds more wrote to clients, used the shell ads provided and took part in local advertorials.

Media coverage of Undiscovered Billions has been outstanding. Every national newspaper bar one covered the campaign in its first two weeks. The BBC made a programme called *Here and Now* based on the issues using IFA Promotion material. The theme they developed was 'Taxbusters'. The findings were also featured in the BBC's *Good Fortunes* programme. The IFA Promotion's chief executive, Joanne Hindle, was interviewed by 30 radio stations.

The Undiscovered Billions campaign shows how solid, yet consumer-oriented research can be used to mount a highly effective and focused campaign which can be rolled out over a period of time. Lansons are capitalising on this approach and will continue the theme in future campaigns.

5

Setting objectives

Knowing where you're going

Setting realistic objectives is absolutely vital if the programme or campaign that is being planned is to have direction and to achieve something.

One of the things that is rife in the public relations industry is over-promising. This applies to both in-house departments and consultancies. It comes partly from an eagerness to please, but largely from a lack of knowledge about what can actually be achieved.

Ultimately the aim of public relations is to influence attitudes and behaviour. You might want to encourage someone to buy your newly introduced furniture range, or keep their holdings in the company, or to speak up for the company when it is under attack. However there are several steps along the way to influencing attitudes and it is only very occasionally that someone who is dedicated to opposing something or who has no particular opinion at all will suddenly become an ardent supporter.

Attitude is all important

According to American academics Cutlip, Center and Broom[1] public relations is about changing or neutralising hostile opinions, crystallising uninformed or latent opinions, or conserving favourable opinions.

Of course one of the things research will have shown is exactly what the attitudes of the various publics or audiences are and this is vitally important when planning a programme. It is a much easier and less time-consuming job to reinforce favourable opinion than to neutralise hostile ones. In fact it may be that we would have to admit that it is impossible to neutralise ingrained opinions, particularly if they are based on deep-seated prejudice or fact.

So, how are attitudes formed? All kinds of influences impact on us:

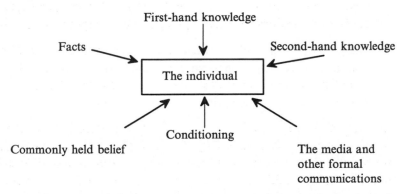

- *First-hand knowledge* is a very powerful attitude former. If you buy a car from a certain garage and the sales and after-sales service has been excellent, you will have a favourable attitude towards them.

- *Second-hand knowledge,* particularly if we gain that from a friend or trusted colleague, is also a strong influence. We may hear from them what a certain country is like and that

[1]Cutlip, S M, Center, A H and Broom, G M (1994) *Effective Public Relations*, Prentice-Hall International Inc, 7th edn.

knowledge coupled with a good brochure, may persuade us to holiday there.

- *The media* is a potent influence, particularly if a topic is one of heightened public interest such as the concern over standards in public life. Companies also communicate via other formal methods such as annual reports and product literature.

- *Conditioning* influences the way we look at and view everything we come into contact with. How we have been brought up, our education, religious beliefs, political views, our age, sex and social position are all part of the baggage we bring with us when thinking about any subject.

- Then there are *commonly held beliefs.* For example, we may believe, even though we may not own one ourselves or know anyone else who owns one, that Aston Martins are superb cars or that Italian suits are especially well designed and made.

- *Facts* also affect our attitudes. Our knowledge that New Zealand is at the other side of the world will make us disbelieve anyone who says they can cycle there in half an hour.

Usually attitudes are formed via a combination of all these factors. Some attitudes are very firmly fixed, like our view of the service we get from our bank, while other attitudes may be much more loosely held, for example our view of the French government (in fact we may not have an attitude towards the French government at all).

The communication chain

To set realistic objectives, apart from understanding what the attitudes of our various publics are, we also need to understand a little about the communication process. Assumptions along the lines of 'If I tell it loud and long and they hear it, eventually they'll believe it' are naive in the extreme.

Real communication involves the two-way exchange of information. However, many public relations practitioners in effect believe that the single-step communication model is what happens in real life:

SENDER ⎯⎯⎯⎯⎯⟶ MESSAGE ⎯⎯⎯⎯⎯⟶ RECEIVER

The idea is that the sender is active, the receiver is passive and that the message is fully understood. What's missing from this model is any notion of feedback. We need to know if our message has affected the receiver at all by changing or reinforcing their attitudes, or making them behave in a particular way. A much more realistic model shown in Figure 5.1.

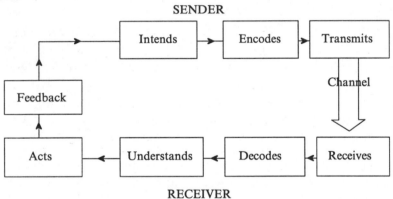

Figure 5.1. *The Communication Process Model*

The sender intends to communicate and articulates or encodes that intention bringing with them all the conditioning baggage mentioned before. They then choose a channel through which to transmit their communication. This may be the spoken word, a page of text or a gesture, and the recipient receives that communication.

The actual transmission of information is fraught with danger. It may be that the message has associated channel noise. The radio may be crackly or the writing may be poorly laid out and difficult to read. There may also be psychological noise. The sender might be using the wrong body language or the corporate message from the chief executive may be intimidating rather than informative. Then there is language noise where the language itself can be misinterpreted. 'Do not cross while light is flashing' can mean do not cross when the light is flashing or do not cross until the light is flashing!

Having once received the message, the recipient then needs to decode it so that it can be understood. They too bring all their conditioning into the decoding equation. There is then normally some sort of action following on from the communication. This might be a simple grunt of recognition or a positive and vehement rejection of the idea proposed, accompanied by a violent gesture. This then closes the feedback loop since the sender is looking for a reaction to their message which demonstrates communication has taken place.

When we are dealing with mass audiences there are many receivers and it is impossible to influence people in a uniform way. People select information depending on their various states of knowledge or depending on their predisposition. Receivers talk to each other, they are influenced by opinion leaders and so on. This recognition has led to the development of the two-step communication model where the information is received by key 'gatekeepers' (normally opinion leaders), who further interpret for the mass audience.

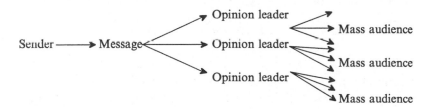

Thus, for example, if a public relations practitioner sends out a press release, the targeted journalists perform the role of opinion leaders and interpret the information on behalf of their readers. Again, some uniformity of interpretation is assumed.

In reality this model is unrealistic too. People receive information from all kinds of sources and this often bypasses the opinion leader. Communication is multi-faceted, multi-step and multi-directional.

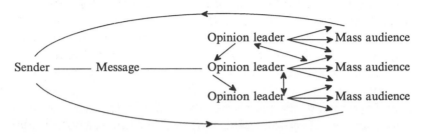

All this communication is overlaid with individual and group attitudes, psychological variables, channel noise, feedback from various sources and the knowledge base of all those involved. Little wonder, then, that communication with mass audiences is an immensely complex and open-ended business.

Work in the communication field in the late 1950s speculated that we seek out information that is in tune with our own attitudes and resist messages that conflict with them. More recent work indicates that people select information because it is relevant to them, not because it reinforces their views. So, if you buy a new personal computer you might find out a lot about the various products available before choosing the one you eventually buy. Having bought the computer you then continue to seek out information about it, not to confirm your choice, but because you want to find out as much as possible about your new machine so you can exploit it to the full.

The key thing is that the receiver is not passive. Many public relations practitioners want to believe in the Domino Theory of the effect of communication.

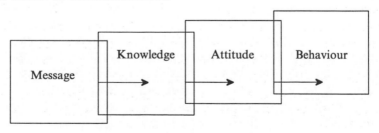

This theory is reflected in early marketing theory which was based on the AIDA model. First of all people become Aware of an idea or product or service but have little knowledge about it. Then they develop an Interest and seek out more information. Then they become persuaded of the benefits of the idea or product or service and develop a Desire to buy it. Finally they show their support by taking Action and buying the product or service.

Sometimes this simple progression is fine, but often it is not. An audience or public might learn about an organisation and form a negative rather than a positive attitude, or they might develop an attitude, but not take the desired action.

The portrayal of wars and famines often engenders strong sympathy in the minds of television viewers and newspaper readers, but they might not make a charitable donation as a result. There is certainly no proven causal link between people thinking about something, forming an attitude and then acting in a predictable way. Public relations people may provide and present in an attractive manner all the information an individual needs to think or act in a particular way. However, the way those individuals form their attitudes and behave is usually very specific to them and their particular situation, and is not entirely predictable.

Furthermore, people are very adept at holding incompatible beliefs and these might change. For example, someone may be a vociferous supporter of measures to combat environmental pollution, but may own a car. They will therefore argue differently depending on the situation they are talking about. One thing is very clear. If someone is very firmly of a particular opinion and acts to support it, it will be very difficult to persuade them to a different point of view. It is not that communication has no effect, but we do need to know where our public or audience stands before we can construct realistic objectives. Just giving people lots of positive information will not necessarily change their attitudes or behaviour. The leverage points (points of weakness in their argument or strength in ours) have to be identified and worked upon in order to produce productive shifts in attitude or behaviour. If there are no leverage points which can be worked on persuasively, the argument is lost from the start.

Setting realistic objectives

Bearing all this in mind then, we can now look at setting achievable objectives. The objective might be quite simply to get someone to think about something (especially if the idea is new or if they are opposed to it). It might be to get them to form a specific opinion (maybe if their views are unformed) or it may be to get them to act, in a specific way (if they are currently supportive anyway). It is a much larger and more difficult task to get someone to act, than it is to get them to think about something.

The objective of public relations programmes is to seek to inform the attitude forming process with the intention that when there is an eventual call for action the targeted individuals or groups are more likely to act in a certain way. The kinds of objectives public relations programmes might have could be to:

- promote understanding;
- overcome misunderstanding or apathy;
- create awareness;
- inform;
- develop knowledge;
- displace prejudice;
- encourage belief;
- confirm or realign a perception;
- act in a particular way.

In the Lansons Communications campaign for IFA quoted in Chapter 4, the objectives of the programme were very clear: to create awareness of the fact that most people did not manage their finances effectively (a key leverage point: people don't like to waste their money); to encourage them to seek professional advice, to inform them that the IFA Promotion hotline was there to help them; and to get them to use it.

Seven golden rules of objective setting

There are seven imperatives that must be borne in mind when setting objectives.

- *Set public relations objectives.* Again it is a tendency of public relations professionals to set objectives that public relations cannot deliver. It is not reasonable to say that public relations should increase sales by 20 per cent. That depends on the salesforce. It is reasonable to say that presentations should be made to 50 per cent of our key retailers to tell them of our new product lines and to try them. It may well be that as a result sales do increase by 20 per cent – but it is outside our control to promise this.

- *Ally to organisational objectives.* Public relations programmes and campaigns must support corporate objectives, otherwise effort will be dissipated on interesting but essentially trivial work. If a corporate objective is a major repositioning of the company in its market, then the public relations effort must be directed to supporting that.

- *Be precise and specific.* Objectives need to be sharp. To create awareness is not good enough. Creating awareness of what, to whom, when and how needs to be clearly spelled out.

- *Do what is achievable.* It is better to set modest objectives and hit them, than to aim for the sky and miss. Wherever possible evaluate the likely benefits of ideas and pre-test or pilot schemes. If a major part of the programme is to contact all investors to inform them of a particular development, you must be sure you can do it within the Stock Market rules.

- *Quantify as much as possible.* Not all objectives are precisely quantifiable, but most are. If you aim to contact particular audience groups say how many. Quantifying objectives makes evaluation much easier.

- *Work within budget.* This goes without saying. It is no good claiming to be creative and therefore not interested in money.

A good planner and manager knows exactly how much things will cost, and will run budget tracking programmes.

- *Work to a priority list.* Public relations people always have too much to do and they could extend their list of activities indefinitely. Know what your priorities are and stick to them religiously. If you do have to work on non-prioritised work, make sure you let your superiors know the consequences of their demands. Prioritising objectives enables you to see where the major effort is to be focused.

  Examples of workable objectives are as follows:

Corporate:	Inform 10 targeted investors of reasons for management buy-out
Trade:	Ensure 50 top dealers attend annual dealers conference
Consumer:	Increase levered editorial coverage of service by 20 per cent
Employees:	Maximise branch acceptance of corporate clothing
Community:	Double job applications from local school leavers

Constraints on objectives

Of course it would be nice to plan without any form of constraint, but there are usually a number of factors that have to be given careful regard. These are either internally or externally generated.

Internal constraints

- *Who should do the job?* The capabilities of the people assigned to the task need careful assessment. Are they able to carry it out? If not, will this mean that the demands of the task will have to be limited? Alternatively, is it possible to enlist the help of other people such as a public relations consultancy? Do you have enough people for the task? Again can extra hands be drafted in or will the scope of the task need to be reduced?

- *How much will it cost?* No one has an open-ended budget so what are the effects on your prioritised programme of any budgetary constraints?

- *When does it need to happen?* Sometimes an internal timetable will require that the public relations task has to be carried out at a certain time, for example, the announcement of a major company restructure or the introduction of a new process.

- *Who makes the decisions?* Are the public relations professionals able to decide on the appropriate courses of action or is the power elsewhere, such as with a marketing director?

- *Is the support in place?* Is there the right administrative back up and physical resources such as faxes, and video conferencing, to support the programme?

External constraints

- *Who are you trying to reach?* What is the range of publics or audiences? How many are there? What is their geographical spread? What about their socio-economic grouping?

- *What are the socio-cultural differences?* What are the different media conventions in the various countries you are operating in? What social and cultural differences have to be observed?

- *What infrastructure support is there?* What facilities such as telephone or access to computers are available?

- *Timeframes?* Are there certain calendar dates such as Christmas or Bonfire Night that have to be met? What about other key events such as the Motor Show or the Ideal Home Exhibition?

Strategic and tactical objectives

Objectives can of course apply to whole programmes or

individual projects. They can also operate at two levels, the strategic and the tactical.

The example below shows how an issue that an organisation faces translates into objectives at both the strategic and tactic level.

ISSUE	STRATEGIC OBJECTIVE	TACTICAL OBJECTIVE
Company seen as backward	Position as company that produces innovative products	Promote this product as innovative
Company not seen as contributor to community	Position as company that takes public responsibility seriously	Promote company sponsored recycling scheme in community
Company not seen as caring employer	Position as company committed to employees	Promote women-returners scheme

The setting of good, realistic objectives is fundamental to the success of public relations plans and campaigns. They provide the whole basis of the programme by clearly setting down what the key achievement must be. They set the agenda for the actions to be taken and provide the benchmark for evaluation further down the road.

The temptation to over-promise must be resisted. That is not to say that public relations practitioners should set themselves soft targets, they should be as rigorous as any other business area. They must, however, recognise the complexity of the communication process, and be realistic about what shifts in attitude and behaviour can be achieved.

Programmes that aim to produce radical shifts in attitude and behaviour will take a great deal of time and are bound initially to meet with a limited amount of success. There are of course exceptions to break the rule, but the most successful programmes start from the point where the audiences are, and attempt to make incremental shifts which, over a period of time, can be seen to have made considerable progress. The reputations of our best companies have taken considerable time to build.

Public relations activity is to do with building reputations too, and that is a slow and painstaking business.

6

Knowing the publics and messages

Who shall we talk to and what shall we say?

Having answered the question 'Where am I going?' by setting achievable objectives, the next question to ask is 'Who shall I talk to?'

By undertaking research for the proposed programme you will already have an analysis of the attitudes of each of the audiences that relate to the organisation. Now these audiences or publics need to have a priority order put on them. Sometimes the priorities are fairly obvious. If you want to launch a new product, the primary audiences are going to be existing and potential customers. However, sometimes the latter grouping is more difficult. Maybe you need to begin to speak to groupings with whom you have had little or nothing to do. If you are a private company seeking a stock market listing then you will need to speak to the city, financial journalists and potential investors, and you will have to begin from scratch.

There are groupings of publics that are fairly common to most organisations. These are shown in Figure 6.1.

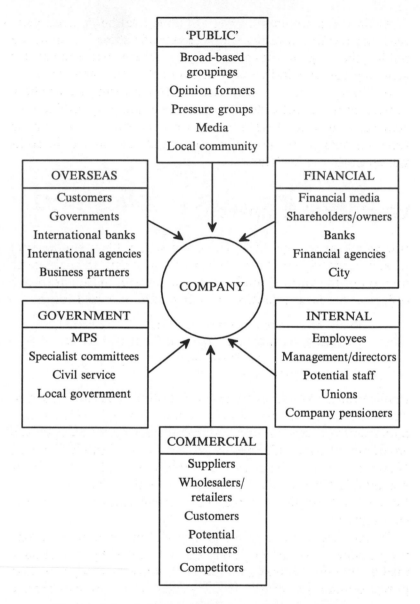

Figure 6.1 *Publics common to most organisations*

Again it is a common failing of public relations practitioners that they perform a rather simple and crude chopping up of the publics that organisations have. They believe that a particular grouping contains individuals who all act in the same way.

In Chapter 5 when we discussed objective setting we saw how radical shifts in attitude and behaviour are very difficult to achieve. It is vital therefore that we understand what can be achieved with particular audiences or publics and the different sub-sections within them.

What is public opinion?

It is worth spending a little time discussing public opinion since what we are trying to do in public relations is shift the balance of opinion of the various publics we interact with in favour of our organisation. One definition of public opinion is as follows:

> Public opinion represents a consensus, which emerges over time, from all the expressed views that cluster around an issue in debate, and that this consensus exercises power.[1]

Public opinion works two ways: it is both a cause and effect of public relations activity. Public opinion, strongly held, affects management decisions. For example, increasing concerns for the environment have affected the motor and furniture industries. Noxious emissions from cars have been cut and trade in non-replantable hard-woods is frowned on. Public relations practitioners publicise the fact that their organisations care for the environment.

On the other hand, a stated objective of many public relations programmes is to affect public opinion, often by mounting a media relations campaign. The commonly held view is that public opinion is 'what is in the media' and if we can change

---

[1] Cutlip, S M, Center, A H and Broom, G M (1994) *Effective Public Relations*, Prentice-Hall International Inc, 7th edn.

what the media says, public opinion will also change. However, as we saw in Chapter 4, implanting an opinion does not always change behaviour.

Most people have opinions on most things, you only have to ask them. The fear of many public relations people is that these opinions could be drawn together and focused by the media against their organisation. The hope is by getting an organisation's message out, mass opinion will be supportive. Thus many public relations programmes adopt a scatter-gun approach, spreading very general messages to very broad publics.

Research in America[1] has found that 80 per cent of people are unaware of key stories in the press. It also found that although politicians said crime was the biggest issue in the country, only 4 per cent of people mentioned crime or violence as the biggest concern for them. Most were worried about making ends meet.

This apparent lack of interest can be very easily explained. Most people have neither the time nor the energy to be involved in everything. They are selective and devote time to those things that they are involved in, and where they feel they can make a contribution.

Uniform public opinion occurs very occasionally and well-informed public opinion occurs even more rarely.

The media do not determine what people think, however they do provide a platform for discussing issues and they can reinforce the 'public' view if a particular issue catches the imagination.

However, what appears to be a small proportion of the total population (for example students) concerned with a particular issue (Third World indebtedness) can be a large group when all banded together and can affect the mission of a business (eg the UK banks).

Opinions are very interesting phenomena and can operate at different levels. Asked for a view of something in the news, most people will offer an opinion. That might be superficial and not

---

[1] Harwood, Richard, 'So what do polls signify?' *Washington Post*, 25 June 1994.

always thought-through. These opinions might be called perceptions. At a deeper level people may have an opinion about a particular issue such as hanging which has been well thought-through and for which they can produce arguments. They can be said to have a particular attitude towards that subject. At an even deeper level attitudes can turn into forms of behaviour. At the most extreme, this could take the form of direct action which could be against the law, such as some of the activities of the more militant animal rights activists.

People can hold two conflicting opinions at the same time. For example they might think animal experiments to be wrong in general, but also believe that certain types of drugs should be tested on animals before being used on human beings.

James Grunig[1] defines three sorts of publics.

- *Latent* which are groups that face a problem as a result of an organisation's actions, but fail to recognise it.

- *Aware* publics, which are groups that recognise a problem exists.

- *Active* publics, which are groups that do something about the problem.

Active publics can be further broken down into three categories.

- *All issue publics* are active on all issues affecting an organisation. For instance that public might be opposed to the organisation in principle and try to disrupt all its activities. An example of this is the anti-nuclear lobby which will oppose the work of any company involved in handling nuclear material.

- *Single issue publics* are active on one issue or a small set of issues – for example the Save the Whale campaign. They might not be opposed to an organisation per se, but will oppose any activity that is contrary to their view on that

[1] Grunig, J E and Hunt, T (1992) *Managing Public Relations*, Holt, Rinehart & Winston, 2nd edn.

particular issue. In fact they may be broadly supportive of an organisation, but totally opposed to one particular activity, such as giving advantageous share options to directors.

- *Hot issue publics* are those involved in an issue that has broad public support which is usually given extensive media coverage. An example of this would be the campaign against the ownership of certain breeds of dangerous dogs.

There are also what Grunig calls:

- *Apathetic publics* who are publics basically unconcerned by all problems and are effectively not a public at all. However, some theorists would argue that these publics are a grouping that should concern public relations practitioners – everyone has the potential to become interested in an issue.

When an organisation or its publics behave in such a way that the other is affected, then a problem or issue arises. Publics, Grunig argues, are created by specific situations and the problems or opportunities they cause. There is no such thing as a 'general' situation or a 'general' public.

The approach of Grunig allows us to define publics for organisations from two angles:

- First of all a public is defined by considering very carefully exactly who will be affected by the policies and activities of that organisation.
- Second, by monitoring the environment it is possible to identify the groups or organisations whose opinion and behaviour will significantly affect the activities of the organisation.

This apparently theoretical approach is useful, since if an organisation identifies its all-issue publics it will pinpoint those who are likely to be the activists on any particular issue. This group will be more easy to identify than the single or hot issue publics, since this will involve predicting the response of all the various publics with which an organisation interacts at any one time.

From this it is clear that active publics are the most likely to use information from public relations programmes as a prompt for their behaviour. They will only be a proportion of the targeted population, however it is important to identify these groups since communication effort should be focused on them.

A further note of caution is needed. Grunig found that the probability of any behaviour related to issues was less than 20 per cent for all but the most active publics and among the most active publics the probability of behaviour relating to the issues was 52 per cent. The importance in researching the attitudes of the various publics; what they think of the organisation and how they act so that we can understand and communicate more effectively cannot be over-emphasised.

So what about the media?

Having earlier played down the role of the media in influencing public opinion, it is obvious that it does have a powerful role in our lives. Here are some general observations.

The media are more likely to create a public when the information is negative. People react against child abuse or cutting down the rainforests.

If the coverage is extensive and the topic catches the imagination it is possible that a hot issue public could be created.

Hot issue publics often react to the thing of the moment without necessarily thinking things through carefully and once media interest dies down, so does theirs. However, if an organisation handles a hot issue badly they could turn hot issue publics into active ones by forcing them to think more deeply about the issues concerned. The growing support for the Maxwell pensioners is a case in point here.

Media campaigns to promote companies are only likely to reach active publics who positively seek out any information about the organisation they are interested in.

The implications for targeting publics

The implications of all this are fairly obvious. Don't waste time on publics that are not interested in what you are doing or saying, but always keep an eye on them just in case. If a public is important to you, but inactive (for example inactive members in a shareholder syndicate), you will have to be very imaginative in attracting their attention to the information you want to give them. Clever writing, good creative photography, eye-catching and relevant headlines will need to be employed. Active publics are the 'communicators' friend'. They positively seek out and want to understand information. It is impossible to keep a low profile with them, however if you don't supply information they will seek it from elsewhere and being active it could be that they will act against you as well as for you.

Don't expect changes in attitude and behaviour from huge numbers of your publics. Only a proportion of your active and aware publics are likely to respond. However they can act as catalysts for change and their power should not be under-estimated.

How to select your publics

Disregard the 'general' public, it does not exist as far as public relations is concerned.

The easiest way to categorise publics is to move from the general to the particular. First of all define broad categories to identify their connections with the organisation. Divide these broad categories into particular groups. This could be done on the basis of geography or the level of activity likely from the group, or on the power and influence of that group.

Prioritise the groups. An example is given in Figure 6.2 (the groupings are very broad, but the principle holds).

GROUPING	PROPORTION OF COMMUNICATION EFFORT REQUIRED	
Corporate		25%
Shareholders (active)	10%	
Shareholders (passive)	2%	
Government ministers	8%	
Opposition front bench	3%	
Senior civil servants	2%	
Customers		25%
ABC1 householders	15%	
Retail shops	10%	
Employees		20%
Executives	4%	
Supervisors	4%	
Shopfloor workers	8%	
Trade unions	4%	
Community		15%
Neighbours	8%	
Schools	4%	
Potential employees	3%	
Suppliers		15%
Raw materials	10%	
Services	5%	

Figure 6.2 *Proportioning out the public relations effort to different publics*

The overall level of activity is likely to be limited by budget.

Identify the gatekeepers or the leaders of the active groups who are likely to interpret information for others or act as catalysts for action. Remember that individuals or groups can belong to more than one category so there needs to be identification and monitoring of the crossovers to ensure that publics are treated equitably, and so that conflicting messages are not transmitted.

What shall we say?

The nature of particular messages will of course vary depending on the nature of the individual campaign of which they are a part. However, every public relations plan or campaign needs to have a set of messages which forms the main thrust of the communication. These messages need to be clear, concise and readily understood.

Messages are important for two main reasons. First of all they are an essential part of the attitude forming process. If publics play back to the originator the message that the originator has initiated, it is a clear indication (a) that the message has been received and (b) that the message has been taken on board and is in some way being used. That may be just as a part of the thinking process, or it may permeate as far as actions.

The second reason messages are important is that they demonstrate the effectiveness of the communication. They are an essential part of the evaluation process. If distinct messages are utilised directly by the press, or if they are repeated in research such as attitude surveys, that clearly shows the messages have been assimilated. It is quite a small step then to see what actions have been taken as a result of the communication.

Determining the messages

There are four steps in determining messages.

- *Step one* is to take existing articulated perceptions. For example it may be that your organisation's products are regarded as old fashioned and this has been identified in earlier research.

- *Step two* is to define what shifts can be made in those perceptions. If in fact your products have been substantially upgraded you need to say that loud and clear.

- *Step three* is to identify elements of persuasion. The best way to do this is to work on the basis of fact. You might be making major investments in upgrading your plant. It could be that there has been a series of new technology initiatives. Maybe BS5750 has been awarded recently. These are all facts that falsify the view that your products are old fashioned.

- *Step four* is to ensure that the messages are credible and deliverable through public relations. It may be that advertising or direct mail should be enlisted to put across a public relations message.

In its campaign to reposition ICL as a voice of authority in the retail services sector, Paragon Communications used research-based market-leading reports of technology in the retail services sector to demonstrate how ICL was making the running on the technology front. The message was clear. ICL understood and provided the right technology solutions for the sector. As a result, in two years ICL moved from 17 per cent of retailers viewing the company as market leader to 38 per cent holding that view.

Messages can be general in nature. Sometimes they have an overall corporate thrust. Ford's message 'Everything we do is driven by you' is a good example of both an advertising and public relations message that was used in all their television advertising.

These general messages are often backed up by very specific sub-messages which may pinpoint a particular piece of information or a specific service that an organisation wants to put across.

For example, the Royal Mail has a main message on its commitment to the local community.

It also has various sub-messages to illustrate the main message 'Royal Mail cares about the community'. Among them are, 'Royal Mail makes charitable donations', 'Royal Mail is a sponsor of events, organisations, people and/or initiatives which contribute positively to the community' and Royal Mail 'is an ethical and responsible company'.

It is of course important that messages do not conflict as people can belong to more than one public. It is perfectly feasible for there to be differences in nuance, but the overall thrust of the messages must be in broad sympathy with each other.

How the message should be presented

The integrity of a message is affected by a whole host of things that determine whether it is taken seriously or not.

- *Format.* How is the message put across? Are there visual images that are associated with it? The care taken with the physical presentation of a corporate identity is a good example of this. The appropriate words, even typeface, must be used to get across the impact of the message. Bold, joking messages often use brash, elaborate typefaces, serious material uses serif typefaces. A financial institution is probably not going to use cartoons to put across a death benefit product.

- *Tone.* Choice of language is very important. All messages need to have careful attention paid to the mood, atmosphere or style that they are trying to portray. The mood might be upbeat or sombre. This point is carefully linked to the format issue.

- *Context.* The context in which a message is seen is vital. If for example you announce your company results on the day a stock market slide occurs, your performance is bound to be affected too.

- *Timing.* It is no use pumping out information about your special Christmas offers if Christmas was last week.

- *Repetition.* Obviously the more often a credible message is repeated, the more likely it is to be heard and picked up. However, there are instances where familiarity breeds contempt and care has to be taken not to repeat messages for the sake of it or they will become devalued.

Of course having control over all these factors is likely to be a tall order. We all have horror stories to tell about how our meticulously timed press release was ruined because of a particular item in the news. Equally, there are always opportunities that suddenly occur which we feel we have to take advantage of even if the context is not the best possible.

Sometimes the choice of media in which a message is relayed is restricted. An annual report is a legal document and some of the information in it is strictly regulated. At other times the message imperative will dictate the communication channel. A product recall dictates that advertising will be used to get the message out as quickly and in as controlled a format as possible.

It is often the case that publics and messages are not given the attention they deserve in public relations programmes. Publics tend to be approached as being large uniform blocks, while all the research to date shows that even groupings with the same name have many sub-groups within them, some of which are active, some of which are not.

A careful appreciation of where a public stands is essential for well-founded public relations programmes.

Similarly, general messages are all very well in themselves, but particular audiences should be served by particular messages if the communication is to do a specific job of work. Vague content in communication brings about vague results. Sharply refined and aimed messages are much more likely to be effective.

7

Strategy and tactics

Getting the strategy right

Devising the strategy for a plan or campaign is the most difficult part of the planning process. If the strategy is right, everything else rolls off the back of it.

Rather than thinking of a cohesive and coherent strategy, many practitioners move straight to tactics, the 'What shall we do?' part of the programme, rather than thinking carefully about how the overall programme should be shaped. They then end up with a fragmented, unfocused effort which lacks any underpinning or driving force.

Strategy, like planning, applies to total programmes as well as individual activities. It's important because it focuses effort, it gets results and it looks to the long term.

What is strategy?

Strategy is the overall approach that is taken to a programme or campaign. It is the co-ordinating theme or factor, the guiding principle, the big idea, the rationale behind the tactical programme.

Strategy is dictated by the issues arising from your analysis of the information at your disposal (see Chapter 4). It is not the same as objectives and it comes before tactics. It is the foundation upon which a tactical programme is built. Strategy is the overall approach you will take to move you from where you are now to where you want to be.

A very clear example of 'strategy' and 'tactics' was demonstrated in the field war conducted by the combined forces which moved against Iraq following that country's invasion of Kuwait (a particularly appropriate example bearing in mind the military origins of the two words):

The objective: to get the Iraqis out of Kuwait
The strategy: according to General Colin Powell was to cut them (the Iraqis) off and kill them
The tactics: pincer movement of ground forces to cut the Iraqis off from Iraq, carpet bombing, diversionary tactics, cutting bridges and so on

Further examples of the relationship between objectives, strategy and tactics are given in Figure 7.1.

	EXAMPLE ONE	EXAMPLE TWO
Objective	Publicise new product or service	Establish market leader perception
Strategy	Mount media relations campaign	Position as industry voice of authority
Tactics	Press conference Press releases Interviews Competition Advertising etc	Research based reports Quality literature Media relations Speaker platforms Industry forums Award schemes etc

Figure 7.1 *Examples of objectives, strategy and tactics*

From strategy to tactics

It goes without saying that tactics should be clearly linked to strategy. When developing a tactical programme all the powers of creativity need to be developed, but there are one or two key factors that should be borne in mind.

- *Use strategy to guide brainstorms.* Strategy should not act as a strait-jacket, but it does help to keep you focused on the job in hand.

- *Reject non-strategic activities.* Brainstorms are marvellous and stimulating, and all kinds of exciting and wacky ideas can emerge. However, no matter how good the idea, non-strategic activities should be disregarded. Don't throw them away completely, as you might be able to use them in a different programme, but if they don't fit in with the strategic thrust of this programme, they need to be put on one side.

- *Relate tactics to strategy and strategy to objectives.* There should be a definite logical progression. Objectives give the overall direction to the programme – what needs to be achieved. Strategy provides the driving force, the 'how to' and tactics give the general programme in detail, what you will do on a day-to-day basis.

- *Test tactics where possible.* It is always advisable to find out as far as possible if a particular tactic will work. You might know it will work because you've done similar things before, in a slightly different context, but you might be treading in new territory. You need to test its feasibility as far as possible. Thus, if for example you want to run a series of competitions in the regional press, you had better contact two or three papers to find out if they are in sympathy with the idea.

Here is a point to bear in mind. If you have carefully thought-through your strategy and it is the right one to use, you should always change tactics before you change the strategy. A strategic review is a major step. It is likely that you are doing something wrong at the tactical level if a programme is not working as it should.

What tactics should you employ?

Of course it would be easy to think up a series of clever ideas and throw them together into some kind of programme. Too often the techniques themselves become the focus of attention rather than the objective they are meant to achieve.

A programme with a variety of publics and objectives will need a variety of techniques.

One way of looking at public relations programmes is to regard them as 'contact and convince' programmes. First of all you identify and contact the relevant target publics, which entails selecting the publics and choosing a channel of communication through which to contact them. Second, you convince them, through the power of your communications messages, that they should think, believe or act in a certain way.

The set of techniques used in a contact programme must reach a sufficient number of target publics and get the message across to them with enough impact so as to influence them in some way. And this must be done at a reasonable cost. So the public relations practitioner needs to select from a menu of activities.

Opposite is a basic menu of the kinds of activities that are available.

Careful choices have to be made about the combination of techniques to be used and the balance between the various activities selected. Each technique has its own strengths and weaknesses. The idea is to select a range of techniques that complement each other and which, when taken as a whole, provide a powerful raft of communication to the target group.

Some examples will illustrate the point. If a company wants to launch a new and highly visual product, such as a new range of expensive cosmetics, it is important that techniques are selected that allow the physical qualities of the product to be

MEDIA RELATIONS	INTERNAL COMMUNICATION
Press conference	Videos
Press releases	Briefings
Articles and features	Newsletters
One-to-one briefings	Quality guides
Interviews	Compact Disk Interactive
Background briefings/materials	
Photography	
Video News Releases	
ADVERTISING (PR LED)	**CORPORATE IDENTITY**
Corporate	Design
Product	Implementation
DIRECT MAIL (PR LED)	**SPONSORSHIP**
Annual reports	Sport
Brochures/leaflets	Arts
Customer reports	Worthy causes
External newsletters	
General literature	
(Also audio-visual material)	
EXHIBITIONS	**LOBBYING**
Trade and Public	One-to-one briefings
Literature	Background material
Sampling	Videos
Demonstrations	Literature
Audio-visual	Group briefings
	Entertainment
CONFERENCES	**RESEARCH**
Event management	Organisations
Audio-visual	Public relations programmes
Literature	Issues monitoring
Entertainment	Results monitoring
COMMUNITY RELATIONS	**CRISIS MANAGEMENT**
Direct involvement	Planning
Gifts-in-kind	Implementation
Sponsorship	
Donations	
SPECIAL EVENTS	**LIAISON**
AGMs	Internal (including counselling)
SGMs	External
Special occasions	
	FINANCIAL RELATIONS
	Annual report
	Briefing materials
	One-to-one briefing
	Media relations
	Entertainment

demonstrated and where there is some opportunity for some two-way communication. Techniques employed might be exhibitions, sending product samples to journalists, factory tours for journalists, brochures with high quality photographs and a coupon response that can be followed up by sending samples, a media campaign with product samples for consumers, special events at retail outlets, advertising and poster campaigns.

In another situation, say where a company chairperson wants to give detailed financial information to some key investors, the visual and tactile aspects would not be so important, neither is the chairperson talking to a mass audience. In this instance it is important that the message is closely controlled, so a media campaign would not be the best method. The methods chosen might be seminars, production of detailed literature and one-to-one or small group briefings. In these instances, the opportunity for one-to-one interaction to check understanding and support would be critical.

Sometimes the type of campaign clearly dictates the selection of techniques. It would be a brave (or foolish) car manufacturer who did not take their new model to motor shows and allow journalists to test drive it.

Likewise, some techniques are more appropriate to certain types of campaigns. In the consumer area stunts and media attention-grabbing, creative ideas are often a part of the programme, but this is not usually the case in serious lobbying campaigns (although sometimes it is).

So, having brainstormed your ideas for your campaign, how do you finally select from the range of techniques that are open to you? There are two tests to apply.

- *Appropriateness.* Will the technique actually reach the target publics you are aiming for? Will they have the right amount of impact? Is this a credible technique to carry the message you are waiting to relay? Will the message get through using this technique? Is it compatible with other communication devices that the organisation is using?

- *Deliverability*. Can you implement these techniques successfully? Can it be done within the budget and to the required timescale? Do you have the right people with the right expertise to implement the techniques?

Having made the decisions about which broad techniques to employ, consideration has to be given to the specific media to use. Thus, if it is decided that an exhibition is a most suitable technique, we then ask which exhibition needs to be attended? Here judgements have to be made on areas such as how many of your target publics attend the list of available exhibitions. There may be a particular sub-set you need to contact. How does the cost compare between the different exhibitions and which is most cost-effective to you? What sort of fellow exhibitors will there be and are they likely to enhance or detract from your reputation? How influential are those exhibitions? Can you afford not to be there? Who attends who is of importance to you, for example the media? What are the logistical practicalities of you attending one as opposed to another exhibition?

To illustrate two different approaches using very different techniques here are two detailed case studies. Both campaigns have been very successful, but they were aimed at very different audiences and therefore required quite different treatments.

Investors In People Week conducted by Northern Lights PR on behalf of the Yorkshire and Humberside Training and Enterprise Councils (TECs)

In July 1994, the nine Yorkshire and Humberside Training and Enterprise Councils (TECs) appointed Northern Lights to carry out a regional campaign to support the national Investors In People Week (17–21 October 1994).

The campaign was to be the first joint marketing initiative with the TECs and would involve working with the marketing manager and Investors In People manager from each of the nine TECs.

Although the Investors In People standard had been established for four years, businesses saw the idea as a 'flag' or 'plaque' to go on the wall – not as a process which could revolutionise business results.

Northern Lights was charged with convincing businesses of the benefits that Investors In People could bring to a company. A key objective was that businesses should make a commitment to Investors In People as a result of the campaign. The TECs recognised that much of the work would be difficult to evaluate. Some companies decide to commit within weeks of hearing about Investors – for others it can take a year or more. Short-term tangible targets were therefore agreed in terms of generating enquiries from companies and achieving a level of media coverage.

With only three months to organise the campaign, which included the July and August holiday period, and an 18-people approval process, Northern Lights needed to be not only creative, but also highly organised and effective teamworkers.

Planning

The nine TECs carried out research into why companies were not committing to Investors. As a result they agreed a brief for the public relations campaign. The key elements were to:

- produce company profiles explaining what Investors is about and the key benefits;
- hold a series of company visits to enable managers to see how Investors works in practice;
- co-ordinate an advertising campaign in the *Yorkshire Post*;
- generate positive coverage in a range of media, including trade press.

Northern Lights carried out research with journalists as to their views on Investors. They commented that Investors sounded a good idea, but it was being promoted in 'official government speak'. They had not been able to make major features out of material produced to date.

The consultancy also approached those organising the national campaign and local campaigns to ensure that regional activities supported and dovetailed into both. Unfortunately very little information was available for the national campaign until just before the Investors In People Week itself.

Northern Lights advised that the campaign should:

- show tangible business benefits;
- bring out human interest angles.

Action

Northern Lights selected ten case studies with the TECs, ensuring an appropriate regional spread for the key media of the region and a variety of industries to maximise trade press coverage.

Northern Lights developed the media campaign: half-day visits were made to each company (having briefed and prepared them in advance). Each visit covered: pulling together tangible benefits of Investors in a way that could be portrayed graphically; interviewing senior and junior members of staff about the personal benefits from Investors; interviewing the manager who had co-ordinated the Investors process to describe the process, the difficulties, how difficulties were overcome and intangible benefits. Whenever possible photographs were obtained to copy and offer to the press (keeping photography costs down).

Northern Lights worked with the TECs, appointing the Hambledon Group to compare company results on Investors companies against non-Investors companies in the region. The results were turned into a report showing astonishingly improved company performance for Investors In People companies and qualitative benefits were highlighted through the case study visits.

The consultancy wrote feature articles for regional media from the same studies, highlighting the benefits to individuals and the companies, and produced graphics showing tangible company benefits. An employee/press launch was held at a leading regional company, Tinsley Wire (Sheffield) Ltd, with key employer bodies as well as media attending. Northern Lights worked with regional daily press and radio programmes to place articles, organise photos and arrange interviews with companies.

The final part of the campaign was to organise a series of Inside Investors visits. Northern Lights approached each company to agree what aspects of the Investors process they could advise on, and then produced a leaflet about the visits for each TEC to mail to their own company contacts.

Northern Lights worked with Teesside TEC's advertising agency to convert an existing campaign for use in the *Yorkshire Post*, as well as creating an advertisement for the visits. This cut down the time and expense of producing entirely new advertisements.

Evaluation

The whole campaign was devised and launched within three months, and included liaising with 18 TEC staff and 15 companies.

One of the greatest achievements of the campaign was the successful co-ordination between nine TECs. The TECs themselves feel the campaign addresses one of the main criticisms about their work – that joint marketing campaigns would make better use of public funds.

In terms of achieving objectives, media coverage was at least 5 times more than the agreed targets and 95 companies in the region have committed to Investors in People as a result of the week's activities. This is despite only one of the Inside Investors visits having been held when the initial evaluation was done.

The Inside Investors visits programme is fully booked with a waiting list for cancelled places. Seventy freefone calls were received in the two weeks around the campaign. Seven regional radio programme interviews were made on the survey results.

Many features highlighting the benefits of Investors appeared in all key daily business press of the region from the *Hull Daily Mail* to the *Sheffield Telegraph* and the *Bradford Telegraph & Argus*. The *Yorkshire Post* carried a key *Business Post* article and used the case studies, graphics and photos for a major Investors In People supplement. All the regional business magazines carried features including *Institute of Directors* and

Chamber magazines. Trade press coverage has included a variety of publications and many more will be using materials in features on training over the year.

There were also the less tangible results. There was considerable TEC satisfaction. Case study material produced by Northern Lights is now being used by TECs in their own publicity material and to support face-to-face meetings with companies.

Under the national evaluation, it was noted that the national campaign had lacked a news focus for the week. The regional TECs believe that the Yorkshire campaign – even though it was on a much smaller budget – did have a news focus to its activities through the survey. Journalists across the region commented on the quality of material, one saying: 'This is the first time I've seen something from the TECs in plain English with a human interest angle.'

The Yorkshire and Humberside TECs are planning a second co-ordinated regional Investors In People Week – regardless of whether a national campaign is held.

Budget

Fees: £10,000. Costs: £10,000, including research, graphic production, photography, design and print of literature and advertisements.

An effective campaign doesn't always cost a small fortune. In a community relations effort costing a total of £25,000, North West Water has raised £225,000 for its Thirsty World charity campaign. Mixing creativity with employee involvement and solid organisation, North West Water is doing much to enhance its reputation.

Thirsty World Campaign by North West Water

WaterAid is the UK water industry charity established in 1981. It helps to provide communities in Africa and Asia with safe water supplies and sanitation – the basis of good health.

March 1994 saw the launch of North West Water's Thirsty World campaign for WaterAid. The objectives of the campaign were:

- to raise £500,000;
- to involve employees in a major community initiative;
- to heighten awareness of WaterAid;
- to encourage teamwork across the company.

The money raised will go to projects in Hitosa, Southern Ethiopia, where women and children have to spend hours each day fetching and carrying water which is often unfit to drink.

Planning

The campaign is the first of its kind for the charity. Dedicated to saving lives, it is led by employees and also involves region-wide community groups and customers. Hundreds of employees have become involved in dozens of events since the launch date. Thirsty World is a well presented and imaginative campaign with its own symbol. It is run by a pragmatic central group of employee volunteers with company support.

The North West WaterAid committee has been restructured to pay more attention to fund-raising and community action and a steering group meets every two months to co-ordinate events. Every six months a Forum meeting is organised to encourage new individuals or organisations to be involved. At the first meeting of employees a variety of fund-raising ideas was produced through brainstorming. At the second, a variety of community groups were brought together to inform and motivate them to fund raise for the charity.

A little branded merchandise was produced to publicise the campaign, and also used as give-aways to encourage fund-raising.

Action

The campaign highlights were as follows.

- To encourage employees to get involved, the £250 Challenge was set up. Teams of employees pledged to raise the money to a deadline. Over 100 employees formed teams to raise money from a range of community events such as treasure hunts, car boot sales and fun runs. One team raised £1000 from a series of events including a dinner dance, various competitions and book sales.

- Major events included 120 employees in teams taking part in a fun day at Lake Vyrnwy in Wales. The employee organising committee also arranged sponsored abseiling, side stalls and entertainment for the public. Local suppliers were involved in donating equipment, with the event raising over £2000. A sponsored walk at Haweswater reservoir in the Lake District raised £5000 from the efforts of nearly 200 walkers. Finally, a golf tournament, supported by senior executives in the company, raised over £11,000.

- Employees are involved in a community outreach pro-gramme, making presentations to schools and community groups about WaterAid. Schools are also involved in events such as a colouring competition at North West Water's environmental classroom near Wigan, and the centenary of their Thirlmere Aqueduct. Here, a team of ten schoolgirls raised money by carrying water from Thirlmere to Manche-ster, supported by North West Water.

- Publicity to community groups is also achieved by individual meetings and supporting major campaigns to Rotary Club and the Girl Guides.

- An appeal to customers at billing time, funded by the company and co-ordinated by the central committee, raises almost £10,000 annually.

- All proceeds from ticket sales at North West Water-sponsored events, including a concert by the Hallé Orchestra and the international WOMAD festival at Morecambe, Lancashire, are dedicated to Thirsty World.

- To increase the income from North West Water's payroll lottery, a leaflet was produced as part of a major internal promotion. The seven months' income raised equalled that from the whole of the 1993–4 financial year.

Measurement
The Thirsty World Campaign has raised over £225,000. North West Water has benefited too, from increased motivation and

teamwork of employees, as well as the positive public relations generated from campaign activities.

The campaign has been recognised externally as the Best Community Campaign in the IPR North West Awards.

Budget

Customer billing leaflet: £15,000. Campaign budget: £10,000. For such a low budget, the campaign has generated a huge amount of funds.

The scope for creativity is well recognised in the consumer public relations field. The launch of Lean Cuisine by Pielle Public Relations in the mid 1980s is a classic and well worth outlining in brief.

Lean Cuisine

The launch of Findus's Lean Cuisine range of 12 calorie-controlled frozen recipe dishes, described by a leading competitor as 'the biggest thing in frozen food since frozen food' was quite a challenge.

The objective set for Pielle was to create awareness and understanding of a new product concept and product range to encourage product trial. At that time healthy eating was moving from the fringe to the mainstream market.

The audience was Britain's female adults who were actively aware of their weight – some 60 per cent of British women diet regularly and making them aware of healthy eating habits was deemed important.

The consumer public relations dimension of the product launch was as follows.

- Small group briefing lunches for national opinion former consumer journalists (sampling Lean Cuisine of course).
- Leanograms – special deliveries of 500 sets of 12 product samples to opinion leaders and journalists so they could test the claims of the press releases.
- Direct mail to Britain's 3000 slimming club organisers.

- The Lean Lecture on healthy lifestyles for organisers and other nutritional advisers (attended by 450 people – all fed on Lean Cuisine).
- Lean Team events around the country which involved product sampling in slimming clubs and in stores.
- Production of the Lean Lifestyle Report on Britain's attitudes, perceptions and changing lifestyle.
- A mailing to GPs consisting of the Lean Diet Plan (which was also used for on-pack promotions), along with details of the medically controlled trials of the diet plan. A plan was also produced for diabetics.

These tactics were directed specifically to the target audience of slimmers, and were part of a comprehensive marketing support campaign covering a broad spectrum of trade and consumer audiences.

The results were:

- consistent, high media visibility;
- 70 per cent product trial among slimming club members with 60 per cent continuing regular repeat purchase;
- 90 per cent brand awareness among the slimmer group and 80 per cent awareness among consumers;
- year one sales of £15 million, 50 per cent above target.

The big 'What if'? Contingency planning

All good public relations plans cater for the unexpected. There isn't room in this book to go into the whole area of crisis management. That subject, along with issues management is dealt with in *Strategic Public Relations*, another book in this series.

However, it is necessary to be prepared for the unexpected at both the strategic and tactical levels. At the strategic level we need a contingency plan in place for one of three possibilities:

- if the reputation of the organisation is damaged;
- if its financial position is jeopardised;

- if its trading operation is interrupted.

These are major crises that require an immediate response and they need planning. Examples of activities that might precipitate such a crisis are new or proposed legislation, product withdrawal, an acquisition or takeover, strikes, an act of terrorism, a factory closure or heavy redundancies.

In some of these situations tightening up on quality control, improving industrial relations or improving the quality of your intelligence gathering processes could help prevent these problems becoming crises. It is the public relations professional's job to look out for the possible problem areas and to ensure that there are plans in place to deal with the communications implications. It will be necessary to liaise with other key people in the organisation such as the chief executive, marketing function, sales/distribution, finance and quality areas, not to mention the lawyers and insurance advisers.

As the public relations professional your tasks will probably include:

- planning for potential crises with others in the company;
- helping to put together a crisis management team and ensuring there is clear communication between members;
- helping to put together the crisis plan;
- initiating 'trial-runs' of the plan;
- keeping the plan up to date;
- training key members of staff to handle the media;
- ensuring media enquiries are planned for;
- putting together key policy statements;
- acting as a part of the crisis management team if required;
- monitoring the results of crises to improve contingency plans.

Of course, at the strategic level, each of the various scenarios will need to be considered in their own right and separate plans of action developed. There will be common areas in each plan, such as the process for dealing with the media, but tailor-made solutions are required for events of such importance.

At the tactical level contingency planning is very much

common sense. This requires a careful examination of each tactic in the programme to find out what might go wrong. Thus, if an outdoor event is planned, what happens if the weather is bad? What if there are accidents or incidents at the event? What if some of the equipment fails? A balance has to be struck between the ideal and the realistic. If you have arranged a fireworks show you don't have another complete display ready just in case, but you do ensure that as much checking is done as possible and you might ensure that one part of the display is kept in reserve and used at the end if all goes to plan. You'll certainly ensure that there are umbrellas available or a covered stand so that people are kept dry.

Planning the strategy and tactics of a campaign is fun. It is challenging and demanding, both intellectually and creatively, but there is something uniquely rewarding about planning and then executing a programme that is well thought out and well judged. Good public relations plans don't just come from the blue, they are the result of much hard work and consideration. To come up with a strategy that works requires a great deal of research and incisive thinking to get to the heart of the matter. Tactics too should be chosen not just because they are imaginative, but also because they are appropriate to the publics towards whom they are directed and because they are without doubt the correct medium to carry the message.

Planning with care puts the practitioner in control. It enhances the probability of success and it ensures that the right things are focused on.

8

Timescales and resources

Timescales

Two things are certain in a public relations practitioner's life. The first is that there is never enough time to do everything that needs to be done – the tasks and possibilities for action are always far greater than the time available. The second is that because public relations tasks often involve other people and the co-ordination of several elements, it always takes longer than you think to get the job done.

There are two interlinked key factors that must be observed when considering timescales. The first is that deadlines must be identified so that the tasks associated with a project can be completed on time. The second is that the right resources need to be allocated so that the tasks in hand can be completed.

Deadlines can be internally or externally imposed. Examples of internally imposed deadlines might be company keynote events such as the announcement of the chief executive's retirement; the announcement of an acquisition; the diaries of the people who might be involved in the public relations programme.

Externally imposed deadlines might be that you have to be

involved in fixed events such as major shows and exhibitions like the Boat Show or the Badminton Horse Trials. There might be calendar dates that have to be worked to like Christmas or Valentine's Day. Then there may be what would be regarded as most appropriate dates. Ideally you would launch your new garden products in the spring when most people start to work in their gardens, but technically you could launch them at any time.

So how do you ensure that deadlines are met? The key thing is to identify all the individual tasks that have to be done in order for a project to be completed. Below is a list of the main elements of a straightforward press conference.

- Draw up invitation list.
- Organise venue.
- Book catering.
- Issue invitations.
- Book audio-visual equipment.
- Write speeches.
- Prepare presentation slides.
- Prepare media packs.
- Follow up invitations.
- Prepare final attendance list.
- Rehearsals.
- Attend conference.
- Follow up.

Each of these elements then needs breaking down further into all the component parts. Thus, for example, a fairly simple press pack might have in it a press release, some background briefing material, photographs, some product literature or a brochure and a specially designed press folder. To put the pack together will include briefing and monitoring designers, printers and photographers, writing the press material, liaising with the marketing department to get the product literature, liaising with senior management to get approval for the material, reproducing the press release and background briefing, collating press packs and organising delivery to the conference.

Critical path analysis

Once having split the project into its individual components, timings have to be attached. A useful technique here is critical path analysis (CPA) which identifies those elements of a programme that involve the greatest amount of time. It is these elements that dictate when a project can be completed. CPA also recognises that more than one task can be undertaken at a time and therefore enables you to work as efficiently as possible. Thus, a critical path for our press packs may be as shown in Figure 8.1.

Figure 8.1 represents a very tight timetable, and assumes that designers, printers and photographers are all available. Sometimes of course they are not. In practice most practitioners will have a number of suppliers they can call on and most projects do not begin from a standing start as shown in the example. However, the principle holds. Several things have to be done to put together a simple press pack, and they need to be carefully co-ordinated and timed with preferably a little contingency at the end (notice a whole day for collation and another one for delivery with an intervening weekend) in case of emergencies. It is also good practice to get as much done as early as possible to give time at the end for any unforeseen problems. It would have been possible to brief the photographer on day 4 and still have the prints back in time to collate the packs, but it would have been pushing things.

Obviously if you are pushed for time and need to complete the task earlier, ways must be sought to shorten some of the critical path activities. It may be, for example, that you decide to use an existing company folder to put your press material in. Or it may be by allocating additional resources and paying the designer to work the weekend, you can produce a folder in a shortened timescale.

If by shortening the crucial path as much as possible the deadline cannot be met, the activity itself must be questioned and an alternative technique selected.

To go back to the use of the critical path, having once broken

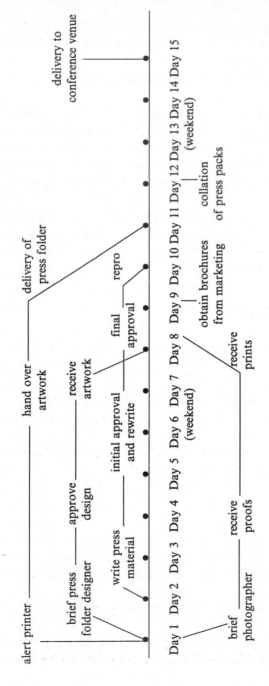

Figure 8.1. *Critical path for putting together a press pack*

down the putting together of the press packs into its own critical path, this can then be put into the larger critical path for the press conference as a whole.

The final programme might look something like that shown in Figure 8.2.

Like any other person, it is important that public relations practitioners manage their time effectively, and work as efficiently as possible by having in place practices and procedures that regularise standard tasks, and by planning ahead. Another book in this series, *A Practitioner's Guide to Implementing Public Relations* by Philip Henslowe, gives a whole host of checklists for typical public relations tasks such as event planning and specifications for suppliers. Checklists are the practitioner's friend and should be used to ensure that everything is done that needs to be done.

Longer-term plans

Putting together plans for individual projects is all very well, but if care is not taken the big picture is lost. It is absolutely essential that the whole campaign or programme is planned in as much detail as possible and an overall timetable for action is constructed. Many practitioners are working to long-term objectives and may have outline plans for several years ahead. Getting those plans on paper and approved is important because it helps maintain a focus beyond the immediate here and now. It is very easy to become so embroiled in day-to-day matters that the strategic vision becomes obscured and overall objectives lost.

Certainly working to at least an annual plan is important. It helps to ensure that things happen when they are supposed to and it gives you control. If other activities arise, you can make a judgement as to whether that or the planned activity should be pursued.

Overleaf is an example of an annual media campaign for a garden centre chain (see Figure 8.3).

It is immediately apparent from Figure 8.3 where the peaks of activity are. February, May and August are going to be heavy

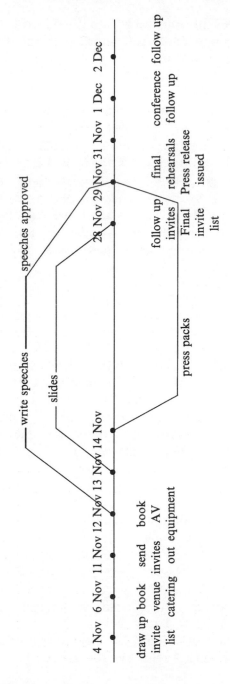

Figure 8.2. *Critical path for press conference*

ACTIVITY	JAN	FEB	MAR	APR	MAY	JUN	JUL	AUG	SEP	OCT	NOV	DEC
EDITOR BRIEFINGS (One-to-one)	Trade press × 2 briefings	Consumer press × 2 briefings	Trade press × 2 briefings	Consumer press × 2 briefings	Trade press × 2 briefings							
Advertorials with key journals (to be negotiated)		*House & Garden*		*Horticultural Journal*		*Garden Answers*		*Horticultural Week*		*Amateur Gardener*		*Royal Horticultural Society Journal*
NEWS STORIES (including new products)	News story	Launch of lawncare advice service	New Centre opening	Launch of tree surgeon service	News story	New Centre opening	Barbecue promotion	News story	New Centre opening	Launch of new power tool range	Christmas plants promotion	New centre opening
SEASONAL THEMES (for regional press)	Tools		Spring is here		Care of fruit trees and bushes		Pest control		Care of borders		Winter lawncare	
Competitions with local press		Power tools promotion			Garden furniture promotion			Water features promotion			Indoor garden promotion	
Exhibitions					Chelsea Flower Show	Gardeners' World		Royal Horticultural Society				

Figure 8.3 *Annual planner for garden centre media campaign*

months, and it might be that extra resources may be needed in the form of consultancy or freelance help.

Obviously a large department or a consultancy carrying out comprehensive programmes will have several activity plans like this covering the whole gamut of public relations work. For example they could well have an internal communications plan, a community relations plan, a business-to-business plan and so on which will all need to be collated into a prioritised master plan. It is then that decisions on resources will be made. Either the plan will be accepted and resourced accordingly or, as is often the case, resources will be limited and therefore activities will have to be cut from the bottom of the priority list upwards. When making decisions on which areas are to be cut, great care has to be taken to ensure that the integrity of the overall programme is maintained and that what remains is a well-integrated programme that provides a good complementary raft of activities which address all the essential audiences.

Resources

Resourcing of public relations programmes comes under three headings. The first is human resources, the second is operating costs and, the third, equipment.

Human resources

Whether working in-house or in consultancy the time and skills of individuals have to be paid for. The more experienced and adept the individual, the more expensive they are. Clearly the level of human resourcing depends on two things: the size of the programme that is to be undertaken and the nature of the programme.

There are tasks that most competent public relations practitioners would be expected to perform. For example, most would be expected to be able to run a media relations programme and produce literature of a good standard. However, highly complex lobbying programmes demand rarer skills and for that you will pay a premium.

A public relations professional with adequate support can run a reasonably broad-based programme of limited depth. Alternatively they can handle a highly focused in-depth programme. The more comprehensive and multi-layered the programme, the more human resources will be required to run it, and the more levels of skill and experience needed.

In an ideal world an optimum programme is devised and justified, and the human resources required allocated. More realistically there is a trade-off between the ideal and the human resource overheads that an organisation is prepared to carry.

However, a real problem comes when human resources are cut. Public relations is a relationship-driven activity and relationships are created by people. By cutting human resources the ability of public relations to do its job is severely threatened. When times are tight, every other avenue for cost cutting must be explored before cutting people. This is a battle that is sometimes hard to win because it is usually the human resource costs that are the greatest in a public relations department. A simple comparison with advertising illustrates the point. An advertising department may have a staff bill of £100,000, but spend £1,000,000 on media. If cuts come their way, it could be possible to cut the media bills by, say, £100,000 without causing irreparable harm. The public relations department may also have a staff bill of £100,000, but its operating costs could be very low because the programme focuses on media relations and internal communications. Costs might be £30,000 or less.

Costs might be saved by trimming the operating budget by the same percentage as the advertising/media cost budget, but the savings will be just £3000. The obvious 'solution' is to cut the human resources where substantial savings can be made. This could spell disaster. Journalists' reasonable expectations might not be met, the internal communications programme may be cut and overall the reputation of the organisation will suffer.

Operating costs

When costing out public relations activities two key things need to be borne in mind: effectiveness and efficiency.

The right techniques need to be selected in order for a programme to be effective. When the techniques have been chosen it is then incumbent on the good public relations professional to be as efficient as possible. So, for example, it might be decided that an effective way to communicate with important customers is via a magazine. Then choices have to be made on such things as format, number of pages, weight of paper and colour content. There is no need to produce a full-colour magazine just because it looks good. If the message content and the right tone can be set by producing a two-colour magazine then that should be the choice. Similarly, if the publication is to be mailed out, the weight of paper will be critical since that, combined with the number of pages, will determine postage costs. Efficient use of resources is important not only from a management point of view, but it may also enable you to undertake additional activities within the same overall budget.

The above examples are fairly straightforward. There are other types of decisions that are less easy and are part of the effectiveness debate. Take, for example, a media relations campaign. Mass mailings of press releases are relatively cheap, but they are of variable effect. Face-to-face interviews can be extremely effective, but are very costly in terms of time compared to mass mailings and you can only reach a very limited number of people. Somewhere in between there are highly targeted mailings, tailor-made to discrete sectors of the press. The same questions of effectiveness and efficiency have to be asked, and the answer will vary depending on the importance of the message and the audience group you are addressing.

Two vital questions need to be asked when looking at effectiveness and efficiency.

Can you get what you want by spending less money?
By thinking laterally it may be possible to achieve exactly the same objective for a fraction of the cost. Examples of this are use of piggy-back mailings. For instance, building societies send out annual statements to members, an ideal opportunity to include additional material.

How about joint ventures with complementary organisations or products? We are all familiar with the washing machine and washing powder link-ups. Then there is sponsorship. It may be possible for you to sponsor an activity that will give you opportunities to raise name awareness or undertake corporate hospitality at a fraction of the cost of putting on alternative activities which are totally funded by you.

At the other end of the spectrum another question on effectiveness needs to be asked.

Will spending a little more add a great deal of value?

Effectiveness does not mean looking to spend the least amount of money all the time; it means getting the most from your money. Sometimes, by spending a little more, a great deal of value can be added. Take a customer magazine. It could also be mailed out to selected press, to shareholders, to the company pensioners just for the cost of a run-on of the print and the postage. The effect could be worth many times the extra cost.

It could be that holding a press conference on site and getting all the journalists there might be more costly, but it could be very much more effective, especially if there are visual elements involved like a new manufacturing process.

Equipment

It goes without saying that a programme or campaign cannot run effectively unless there is the right sort of equipment to support it. Public relations professionals do not require vast amounts of capital equipment, but it is important that it is up to date. Communication professionals need access to, and use of, technology appropriate to their needs. Video conferencing, use of the World Wide Web, desktop publishing and electronic mail were all new technologies once, but they are now just a part of the battery of communication channels that can and should be used.

A note of caution should be sounded. When working on or with international programmes it is easy to assume that every country has ready access to new technologies. This is of course not the case. It is important therefore not to become wholly dependent on new technology.

In summary, when drawing together a budget these three factors must be borne in mind. An example of the main budget headings for a public relations programme is given below.

Budget headings

Human	Operating costs	Equipment
Staff salaries Employment costs Overheads and expenses (eg heat, light, office space)	Print and production Photography Media relations Conferences, seminars, sponsorship etc Operating expenses (eg fax, telephone, stationery, post)	Office furniture Computer equipment and consumables Telephones, fax machines etc

These costs are basically the same whether working in-house or in a consultancy. However, when employing consultancies the salaries element is obviously different. You will pay fees for the programme agreed upon.

These fees will normally be split into two sections.

Advisory fee
This covers consultancy advice, attending meetings, preparing reports etc. This is often based on a fixed amount of time per month.

Implementation fee
This covers the amount of executive time required to implement the agreed programme or campaign. For on-going programmes this is again often based on a fixed amount of time per month, the idea being that some months more time will be devoted to the programme than others, but the work evens itself out in the end as far as payment is concerned.

Some clients prefer, however, to be billed for the actual amount of time spent, particularly if implementation includes a fair amount of project work which requires a variable amount of input from the consultancy.

You will often pay a 'mark-up' on bought-in services such as photography and print where the consultancy has a legal and financial responsibility for client work (the Public Relations Consultants Association (PRCA) recommend 17.65 per cent to cover things like indemnity insurance). You will usually have to pay value added tax (VAT) unless the consultancy is very small and not registered.

A typical monthly invoice from a consultancy might look as follows:

Invoice Headings

		£
PR	Executive time (35 hours at £65 per hour)	2275.00
	Photography (for product launch)	540.50
	Photography (for in-house magazine)	742.70
	Design, artwork and print for magazine	2450.00
	Design, artwork and print for schools pack	3820.00
PR	Operating expenses (fax, phone, stationery, post)	408.00
	Travel (day return to London and subsistence)	54.00
		10290.20
	VAT at 17.5%	1800.79
		12090.99

Overall budgets will be the subject of negotiation. There are, however, two main approaches to budgeting. The first is to adopt a formula approach that applies company-wide so as to determine the proportion of resources allocated to each function. Typical formulae that are applied are a percentage of the organisation's profits or sales turnover, or a fixed increase on the first year's budget or a sum comparable to that of the closest competitor. The main problem with this approach is that it takes no real account of the actual job of work that is required from public relations. The year ahead may involve a great deal of public relations input, for example if the organisation is to mount a major customer care campaign. The range of publics to be contacted varies from organisation to organisation. For some organisations, public relations as opposed to other forms of marketing communication may be the largest or even the only means of promotional activity.

An alternative approach is to start with the tasks that public relations needs to perform, cost them and negotiate the budget on the basis of what is required. This does not give *carte blanche* to the public relations professional, since it is likely that each activity will be carefully scrutinised and will need to be justified. Wherever possible a cost:benefit analysis should be provided to support public relations expenditure.

In most instances a mix of these two approaches is taken. Generally speaking an initial indication of the overall budget available will be given, the practitioner will then put together a detailed plan with costings attached and the final budget will be negotiated.

Should the proposed budget prove unacceptable, some of the activities suggested will have to be cut or their scope narrowed. Inevitably compromises will have to be made, however, carefully detailed plans will demonstrate the consequences of cuts or indicate a list of essential activities, as well as itemising the benefits of the full programme.

9

Knowing what you've achieved: evaluation and review

Measuring success

Public relations is no different from any other business function that you spend money on. You want to know if you are getting value for money. You need to know how successful you've been and if you've not been as successful as you thought you should have been, you need to discover why.

The first thing to do is define the terms. **Evaluation** is an ongoing process if you are talking about long-term programmes. Thus, you will regularly evaluate the media relations element of your programme by making a monthly, critical analysis of your media coverage. As a result of this you may focus more effort on particular messages or journalists.

Similarly, at the end of a specific campaign, you will evaluate the result. So if the objective was to prevent the closure of a factory, you will have a clear cut indication of the result at the end! You've either succeeded or failed.

Review applies to longer term programmes. It would generally be extremely sensible to take a long, hard look at the programme each year. You will look at what the evaluation over the year has shown you, revisit the programme objectives and scrutinise the strategy. It could well be that you carry on as before, but it may be that you will want a complete reorientation of the programme. We will return to this later.

On shorter campaigns you might have to undertake a review if the strategy and tactics are clearly wrong because the campaign is not working.

In a nutshell, evaluation is a monitoring and tweaking process, while review is a step back to identify any strategic changes that need to take place.

In 1994, the top ten European consultancies earned £203 million[1] in income. The top ten UK consultancies earned £103 million[2] and the largest ten UK in-house departments had budgets totalling about £39 million.[3]

It is no wonder then that clients and companies are keen to know what public relations is doing for them.

The benefits of evaluation

It could be that evaluation is viewed as a great chore, best avoided if possible because it means that your head is on the block. But why shouldn't you be accountable? Most people are. Dishwashers are meant to produce clean dishes and advertising professionals are meant to generate sales; public relations professionals are not a privileged élite doing high and lofty things that are far too important or intangible to measure.

If undertaken properly, evaluation actually puts you in the driving seat. It helps you spot danger signs before real problems

---

[1] 'PR Week Top European Agencies', *PR Week*, 28 July 1995 (owned groups, not networks).
[2] 'PR Week Top 150', *PR Week* 28 April 1995.
[3] 'PR Week In-house PR survey, *PR Week*, 30 June 1995.

develop and it helps you prove your worth. Here are a few reasons why you should build evaluation into your campaigns and programmes.

- *It focuses effort.* If you know you are going to be measured on a number of key agreed targets, you will focus on the important and keep the secondary in perspective.
- *It demonstrates effectiveness.* There is no success like success! If you achieve what you have aimed to achieve, no one can take that from you. You can prove your worth.
- *It ensures cost-efficiency.* Because you are concentrating on the things that should take priority, you will spend your budget and your time (which is also money) on the things that count and achieve the big result.
- *It encourages good management.* Management by objectives, having clear goals, brings sharpness to the whole public relations operation. The irrelevant will be quickly identified and rejected.
- *It facilitates accountability.* Not only your accountability to produce results, which is perfectly in order, but it also makes other people accountable in their dealings with you. You can quite legitimately say 'If I spend time doing this unscheduled project, it means that I cannot complete this planned activity. Which is more important?' Then clear choices can be made about what may be new and pressing priorities. If the planned activity is also essential, then you might need extra help – so you are in a powerful position to ask for more people or extra budget.

Why practitioners don't evaluate

In a survey[1] of IPR members' attitudes to evaluation, Tom Watson discovered that while three-quarters of practitioners

---

[1] Watson, T (1993) 'Output measures rule in evaluation debate' *IPR Journal*, vol 12, no 5, November.

claimed to undertake some form of evaluation, three-quarters of respondents also agreed that little money was spent on evaluation – from zero to 5 per cent of total budget.

When questioned about their motives for undertaking evaluation, 'prove value of campaign/budget' came out a very clear leader, followed by 'help campaign targeting and planning' and 'need to judge campaign effects'. Another reason, 'help set more resources/fees', came a distant fourth.

Watson's research showed that practitioners were defensive about their activities. They used evaluation techniques to present data on which they could be judged rather than using evaluation to improve programmes.

Output measurement was seen to be more relevant than gauging impact or gaining intelligence so that programmes could be improved.

He also pinpointed the main reasons why programmes were not formally evaluated. These were, first, lack of knowledge (possibly disinclination to learn about evaluation techniques), second was 'cost', followed by 'lack of time' and 'lack of budget'. When added together, 'cost' and 'lack of budget' became the dominant reasons.

There are other reasons why evaluation is seen to be problematic.

- *Understanding what it is that has to be evaluated.* Often what is measured is output not outcome. So we will be very happy to see a nice, fat clippings file and will spend money to pay a clipping agency to collate the file for us. We may even do some more sophisticated form of analysis like trying to measure the worth of a clipping depending on its position on the page, its size, the number of key messages it contains and so on. There are several companies that provide such a service. Some will provide a more detailed analysis, for example, a breakdown of how many times specific publications or journalists used your press releases and the types of treatment your story received.

    However, in the long run it doesn't matter how heavy the clippings file is, what matters is what those clippings achieved (the outcome). As a result was there a 20 per cent increase in attendance at the AGM? Has the attitude of your key public altered?

- **Setting objectives.** Objectives need framing in measurable terms. 'Raising awareness' is not a good objective unless you quantify by how much: 1 per cent or 99 per cent? Research will show you what is possible. Some objectives will be fairly simple to quantify. A campaign to change a law will either succeed or not, or it may be partially successful. There is also likely to be a set timeframe over which to work. A long-term campaign to change the general attitude towards the decriminalisation of drugs is likely to have patchy, incremental results over a long period. However, even in this situation it is possible to lay down clear benchmarks. For example, a legitimate objective would be to persuade the majority of chief constables by the year 2000 or give up the campaign.

  The achievement of objectives is the clearest way to evaluate any programme or campaign.

- **Understanding what can be achieved.** Public relations practitioners should make realistic promises. It is just not possible to get the chief executive on the front page of the *Financial Times* every month unless he or she or the organisation is exceptional in some way (or notorious!). What is required is an honest, sober appraisal of what can be achieved. That knowledge comes with good research and the benefit of experience. Managing expectations is a key practitioner task.

  The over-promising problem is exacerbated by a genuine lack of knowledge of the psychological art of the possible. As detailed in Chapter 5 it is very difficult or at least will require a very determined and fact-filled campaign that will convert people who have a fixed view to take on the opposite view. It is a less onerous task if the target public has no view at all, or if they are reasonably well disposed because your message confirms or fits in with their own desires or views. Again research will identify audience attitudes and therefore the size of the public relations task.

- *Range of evaluation techniques required.* Public relations is unlike some other forms of marketing communication, such as direct mail, where the evaluation is relatively simple. You count the number of returns and the business transacted. Public relations addresses many audiences in many different ways and different types of evaluation technique are needed.

- *The communication chain.* The decisions that have to be taken all along the communication chain affect the communication outcome. You have to decide on the message, the medium, the form of words and/or images, and ensure the target is receiving and interpreting the communication correctly. 'Evaluation' has to take place all along the chain. If one element is wrong, the desired outcome will not be achieved. Thus evaluation just at the end of a programme can be misleading.

It is impossible in this book to give an evaluation blueprint for every type of public relations activity. For some activities evaluation will be quite easy. If, for example, you are running an exhibition stand it is a simple, quantitative exercise to count the number of product enquiries, take contact addresses and then trace back subsequent product orders.

Other things like the effects of a long-term sponsorship programme are much more difficult to evaluate.

An evaluation model and some other measures

A useful device is the macro-model of evaluation demonstrated by Jim Macnamara[1] (see Figure 9.1). The model forms a pyramid. At the base are inputs, basically information and planning, and at the peak, objectives achieved. Each activity is split down into the various steps of the communication process.

---

[1] Macnamara, J R (1992) 'Evaluation of public relations. The Achilles heel of the PR profession', *International Public Relations Review*, vol 15, November.

It recognises inputs and asks the user to make a judgement on the quality of information, the choice of medium and the content of the communication. It then considers outputs, that is the communication produced, for example, the newsletter, the press release, the brochure, and then it considers the results or outcomes – what the communication actually achieved. Alongside the steps is a list of evaluation methods that might be used for a media campaign, a newsletter and so on.

The model needs to be customised for each project, but the basics remain the same. Its strength is that it recognises a range of evaluation methods; there is no all-embracing magic formula.

The more advanced evaluation methods further up the pyramid are recommended. They measure actual outcomes. They are more sophisticated and of course more expensive. The ones lower down the pyramid are more basic and can be seen as tests that you are doing things right, more akin to quality control. However, these basic checks are not to be missed. You can be more confident of success higher up the pyramid if you get the basics right.

In practical terms how does this translate into reality? There are a number of critical factors to consider when planning a campaign or programme:

- set measurable objectives;
- build in evaluation and quality checks from the start;
- agree measurement criteria with whoever will be judging the success of your work;
- establish monitoring procedures that are open and transparent, for example, monthly reviews of progress;
- demonstrate results.

Typical objective measures that might be employed are:

- changes in behaviour (for example if a product is given public relations support, buyer behaviour can be tracked);
- responses (return of reply-paids, response slips, salesforce quotes etc);

143

EVALUATION OF PUBLIC RELATIONS PROGRAMME

STAGES	ACTIVITIES	METHODOLOGIES
RESULTS	Objective achieved or problem solved	• Observation (in some cases) • Quantitative research
	Number who behave in a desired manner	• Sales statistics, enrolments etc • Quantitative research
	Number who change attitudes	• Qualitative research (cognition acceptance)
	Number who learn message content (eg increased knowledge, awareness, understanding)	• Qualitative research
	Number who consider messages	• Readership, listenership or viewership statistics • Attendance at events • Inquiry or response rates (eg coupons, calls)
	Number who receive messages	• Circulation figures • Audience analysis
	Number of messages supporting objectives	• Analysis of media coverage (Breakdown positive, negative and neutral – eg Media Content Analysis)
OUTPUTS	Number of messages placed in the media	• Media monitoring (clippings and broadcast media tapes)
	Number of messages sent	• Distribution statistics
	Quality of message presentation (eg newsletter or brochure design, newsworthiness of story)	• Expert review • Feedback • Audience surveys • Awards
	Appropriateness of message content	• Readability tests (eg Gunning, Flesch, SST) • Case studies • Pre-testing • Review • Pre-testing (eg focus groups)
	Appropriateness of the medium	
INPUTS	Adequacy of background information, intelligence, research	• Review • Existing research data • Benchmark research

Figure 9.1 *Macnamara's macro-model of evaluation*

- changes in attitude, opinion, awareness – especially important for opinion-former work (can be measured through telephone research, questionnaires, one-to-one interviews);
- achievements (for example 80 per cent of retailers came to promotional conference);
- media coverage, content, distribution, readership, share of voice (content analysis, readership data);
- budget control and value for money.

It is sometimes relatively easy to put in checks when measuring the effectiveness of editorial, if you work in conjunction with other marketing colleagues. For example, the author was able to place some editorial material next to a financial product advert that had been running for a few weeks in the *Sunday Times*. The number of policies that came from the two adverts previous to the editorial were 27 and 21 respectively. The advert with adjacent editorial resulted in 94 policies being sold from coupons.

Similarly, for another financial product it was found that adjacent editorial doubled the coupon returns from a series of adverts in the *Sunday Telegraph*.

Apart from quantitative objective measures, subjective measures of performance are also quite legitimate. They are the icing on the cake and often put the fun into working in what are often the quite stressful conditions of day-to-day public relations life. These factors may be especially important in the client/consultancy relationship, but are also highly prized in the relationships that in-house departments build with other departments within their organisation. In fact it is often these subjective yardsticks that win business for consultancies (all things being equal) and win ready co-operation from other departments:

- enthusiasm;
- efficiency and professionalism;
- creativity;
- initiative;
- an instinct for what is right in a given situation (based on judgement gained through experience);
- people chemistry.

A critical part of the evaluation process is the effective deployment of both staff and budgets. Regular rigorous monitoring of both is required.

Staff need to be regularly developed to cope with and exploit the rapidly changing communication environment. It is also essential that public relations staff are well motivated and well directed. They are, after all, the handlers and managers of the organisation's reputation in a most overt sense.

If they do not believe in what they are doing, how can they do their job proficiently and professionally?

Likewise, the management and effective use of budgets is a duty laid on every manager. With so many options open to them on how to spend what is often quite a limited budget, the public relations professional must have a keen regard to the careful stewardship of the resources at their disposal. Every pound should count. Chapter 8 gives a more detailed exposition on how budgeting can be done effectively.

Reviewing the situation

While evaluation takes place on an on-going basis, a thorough review takes place less often. As explained earlier (Chapter 4), a major review including extensive research may well take place before a programme or campaign is put in place. That will entail a close examination and analysis of both the external and internal environments, as well as all the aspects of constructing a viable plan as outlined in this book.

Again, all good managers undertake a regular review of their programmes. A long look every 3, 6 and 12 months ensures that everything is on track, and that any new situations are taken into account. Minor modifications can be made as the programme progresses.

The six-month and/or annual review will need to be tough and may involve examining new or on-going research. A day or couple of days away from the office with colleagues who are working with you is time well spent to ensure that all is in order.

There are, however, a number of external and internal

'drivers' that might force a review of a programme or campaign, or indeed its complete abandonment in mid-stream.

While it is essential to tweak tactics as a plan unfolds, especially in the light of information that on-going evaluation brings, the plan itself should remain essentially unaltered. That is because the objectives remain the same and the strategy holds good. However it is essential to bear in mind that public relations is conducted within a dynamic environment and there must be the capability to respond as soon as possible, either in a proactive way to lead or forestall events, or in a reactive way to deal with an emergency situation. A review is required if the overall objectives need to be changed or if the strategy is seen not to be working. Let's deal with the strategy issues first.

Help, the strategy's not working!

If the underlying strategy for a programme or campaign turns out to be wrong, this is a very serious business. To get the strategy wrong indicates fundamental flaws in research or the interpretation of research. An example will illustrate. Suppose a company wants to launch a new product and the public relations strategy is to mount a media relations campaign including a press launch with product demonstrations, merchandising packs for the regional and consumer press, competitions, consumer offers and a couple of stunts designed to attract attention.

Suppose after all this, the product doesn't sell at all well. There are a number of explanations and here are just a few!

- The product is sub-standard. As soon as the public relations professional becomes aware of this they must advise the company accordingly. If they do, but the company insists on going ahead, at least they were told. The damage to long-term reputation could be severe.
- The product is a 'me too' and has no distinguishing features. No amount of good public relations will persuade people to buy this type of product rather than their current favourite, unless of course there are brand strengths. Public relations should not over-promise.

- The product and the message are aimed at the wrong target markets. There is a major flaw in research.
- The message is not accepted. It could be you're saying the wrong things, or in the wrong way, or that the medium or the timing is wrong. There is lack of research or misinterpretation of information.
- The product needs to be sampled by consumers for them to really appreciate it. Then why choose media relations as your main communications vehicle?
- The press aren't interested. You haven't found the right media hook: you aren't approaching them in the right way. It could be lack of research. Maybe another big consumer story is breaking at the same time as your launch. Oh dear! Sometimes all the market intelligence and research in the world can't protect you from this nightmare. In this case your strategy may even be right, but you'll have to change either that or your tactics quickly to get back on the front foot again. Creativity counts.

If the strategy is not working you need to ask two questions.

- *Are my objectives right and realisable?* If the answer to that is 'no' then no wonder the strategy's not working. If the answer is 'yes' then a second question is necessary.
- *What's wrong with the strategy?* What basic point have I overlooked or misinterpreted? This means a return to the research and a careful analysis. Did you ask the right questions in the first place? Did you ask them all? What do the unanswered questions really tell you? Do you really understand your public and what can be achieved? Do your messages have credibility and can they be delivered via the tactics you have plumped for? Is the programme too ambitious or perhaps not sufficiently ambitious? Is the programme adequately resourced?

It is embarrassing to say the least to get the strategy wrong and tactics should always be examined first to see if it's them that is at fault. If you've done careful research and are confident of your interpretation, it is likely to be the tactics, not strategy, that need correcting. However, as with all things, it is better to admit when something is wrong and correct it, rather than limping along wasting time and resources, and damaging your professional reputation.

External and internal review drivers

Through the regular evaluation and review process, adjustments will be made to your campaign or programme. Objectives might be refocused or given a different priority and tactics may be changed. This is part of being effective and in tune with changing requirements. Minor ongoing changes can be expected. However, all the best-laid plans are subject to major review or even reversal if there are fundamental changes in the external or internal environment that cause the objectives of a public relations programme to be changed. Thankfully these 'drivers' occur relatively infrequently, but it is wise to have contingency plans ready to deal with them if or when they do arise, because they usually require some pretty fast-footed action and you may only have one shot at getting it right.

The list below gives a flavour of the sort of external drivers that could force a review:

- legislative change that either threatens or gives expanded opportunities to the organisation;
- competitor activity, which threatens or gives opportunity;
- takeover or acquisition (note, if a company is taken over through a hostile bid it then has to switch its public relations activity from actively campaigning against the acquirer to work for the new owners);
- major product recall or damage to corporate reputation;
- action by a well-organised, powerful, opposing pressure group.

Internal drivers can also make a review essential. The kinds of scenarios that would force this are:

- corporate restructure with new priorities, which may entail the splitting up or restructuring of the public relations function;

- changes in key personnel such as the chief executive (or the director of public relations!);
- budget changes, meaning that public relations activity is significantly cut or expanded;
- future needs. A programme or campaign may end or run out of steam. A fresh look is then required to reactivate and refocus the public relations work.

Once having decided on a review, the planning process then begins its cycle again. Figure 3.2 on page 53 outlines the process. Again the basic questions have to be addressed.

- What are you trying to achieve?
- Who do you want to reach?
- What do you want to say?
- What are the most effective ways of getting the message across?
- How can success be measured?

By systematically working through these questions, all the essentials of planning and managing a successful public relations programme will be covered.

And finally!

This book has given you the basic framework for putting together a well-founded public relations campaign.

Careful, systematic planning will make your life so much easier. Add one more vital ingredient – flair, ability to think outside the square and your work in public relations will be immensely rewarding. There is nothing more exciting than seeing a communication programme buzz and take on a life that can only come from the sort of work the public relations professional does. Communication is about making contact, developing relationships, building trust and achieving results that add to the success of your organisation because the key stakeholders support you. Careful planning and management lies at the heart of that.

Good planning and good luck!

Index